Cambodian History

*A Captivating Guide to the History of
Cambodia and the Khmer Empire*

Free Bonus from Captivating History
(Available for a Limited time)

Hi History Lovers!

Now you have a chance to join our exclusive history list so you can get your first history ebook for free as well as discounts and a potential to get more history books for free! Simply visit the link below to join.

Captivatinghistory.com/ebook

Also, make sure to follow us on Facebook, Twitter and Youtube by searching for Captivating History.

Contents

Part 1: History of Cambodia

A Captivating Guide to Cambodian History, Including Events Such as the Rise and Decline of the Khmer Empire, Siege of Angkor, Cambodian-Vietnamese War, and Cambodian Civil War

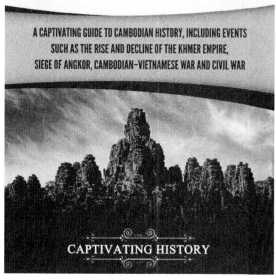

Introduction

Cambodia was, and still is, a country in crisis. At its height, it had a thriving economy, but today, it is tenuous. The people were once well fed, despite having to deal with a cycle of torrential rains during the wet season and spells of dry weather. However, today, the country depends upon the generosity of international donors and help from the United Nations. How did this happen?

Cambodia, or Kampuchea as it was sometimes called in history, was a frequent battleground for other countries besides its own. Still, it had much to call its own. Cambodia had carefully irrigated farmlands and drainage systems, along with systems to provide water during the dry periods. As early as the 12th century, it had hospitals that treated its people with natural medicines and remedies. They had a vigorous maritime trade, canals, and even floating cities, from where they sold their products all over the country. They had a strong empire to call their own—that of the Khmer Empire. It is remembered as one of the greatest societies on the Indochinese Peninsula.

Unfortunately, the majority of the folklore of the olden days has been all but forgotten, with their legends fading into the dust of history. Even the names of some of the revered kings of Cambodia have sunk into anonymity. It perhaps doesn't help that Cambodia's early history wasn't recorded by the Cambodian people themselves; they were related second-hand by traveling traders from China. Historian Claude Jacques (1700–1750) said, "Very basic historical mistakes have been made" in regards to Cambodian history because its history prior to the 12th century was based on Chinese inscriptions. When new inscriptions were found, researchers preferred to adjust the newly discovered facts to the initial outline rather than call the Chinese reports into question.

But why didn't the Cambodians record their own history in a more coherent fashion? These were people who battled with the seasons, which fluctuated from monsoons to parched dry periods. What's more, they were badly in need of good management and an orderly society. They had that for a while under some of their early kings. To exacerbate matters, though, it seems they were "surrounded by assassins," as other leaders and neighboring countries had their own hidden agenda.

Victimized for years by antagonistic neighbors, the Cambodians begged for help from France. They were then betrayed by their beneficent French protectors, who turned tyrannical. But why and how did that happen?

It is up to the reader to determine whether Cambodia was a country bent on achieving power and privilege for itself or a suicidal civilization bent on its own self-destruction in hopes of attaining a utopia of its own making.

Chapter 1 – Early History of Cambodia

Prehistory and Early History

Laang Spean Archaeological Site

Hoabinhian stone tools were found by archaeologists from the Franco-Cambodian Prehistoric Mission in a cave in northwestern Cambodia. Carbon dating tests estimate they date back to 6000 or 7000 BCE. Hoabinhian refers to a geological period when the glaciers were first receding, which would allow for human habitation. These Hoabinhian artifacts include "flaked" tools, with stones having been chipped or scraped to produce points. Prehistoric pottery was also found there, dating back to 4200 BCE.

Area of Archaeological Site at Laang Spean (Yellow)

Samrong Sen Site

Stone Implements and Ceramics at Samrong Sen

At the base of Tonle Sap, a huge lake in western Cambodia, flows the Stueng Chinit River, where several excavations have been conducted by local villagers and the French protectorate of Cambodia in the mid-19th century. A 20th-century excavation yielded prehistoric implements that date to between 3400 BCE and 500 CE. Two of the excavations yielded artifacts, which included armbands, beads, undecorated pottery, and drinking vessels. Skulls and human bones were also discovered, which have been dated to 1500 BCE.

Phum Snay Site

The archaeological site of Phum Snay was discovered in northwestern Cambodia and was excavated by the Australian National University. It is believed the site was first active in the year 500 BCE and fell into disuse around 500 CE. The researchers from the university discovered human remains in a number of burial sites, along with bronze artifacts and semi-precious stones.

Skeletal remains show signs of cranial injuries caused by blunt force trauma, suggesting that this site may have housed a number of warring villages. Some bodies were simply stretched out and placed in pits, while others were buried with ceramic vessels and decorative items, such as rings and bells. Animal bones were also found buried in the dirt, and it was suggested by historians that this may imply sacrificial slaughters of animals accompanied the burial rites. In the graves, iron and bronze tools were found in addition to weapons, which included daggers, swords, spearheads, and other projectile points.

There was also evidence of dental caries (tooth decay) in the human remains. This gives researchers a glimpse into the dietary habits of these early people. It's interesting to note that there was a difference between the males and the females, as the female remains often had more cavities. Researchers have theorized that the males tended to eat more protein-based food, while the females ate more "cariogenic" foods, that is, more starch and carbohydrates.

It has been suggested that the reason behind this was the fact women spent more time working in the fields near the vegetable crops while the men were out hunting.

DNA studies of the human remains found at Phum Snay resemble that of modern-day humans from not only Cambodia but also Thailand, Vietnam, and Laos. According to the journal *Anthropological Science*, examinations of the skeletal remains uncovered at Phum Snay reveal the dental features of the skulls were akin to those of Austronesian ancestors, but some show other evidence of origins from populations farther north, even as far north as Tibet.

Oc Eo Site

This site, now located in Vietnam, was once part of Cambodia. At that site, archaeologists unearthed tools, jewelry, casts for making jewelry, coins, and religious statuary. The coins appear to be imitations of the kind used by Rome during the 1st century, so it has been conjectured that the ancient Romans traversed the area on their way to China, where they sought to open up diplomatic relations.

Scholars indicate that Oc Eo was also a cultural and economic area essential for early Funan development (Funan was an early kingdom that covered parts of Cambodia, Thailand, and Vietnam). There, it was said, traders and craftsmen met and exchanged goods and taught the locals various skills.

Ethnic and Language Groups in Ancient Cambodia

One of the factors used in determining the identity of ancient or indigenous cultures of a region is language. Sanskrit was the classical language of the countries in Southeast Asia. It originated in the Indian subcontinent, the heart of Hinduism and Buddhism. Sanskrit was mostly a spoken language at that time, but it became a written language in the 1st millennium BCE, at least according to surviving evidence. Other language families of Southeast Asia in ancient times were Indo-Iranian and Indo-Aryan. Indo-Aryan is a subgroup of the Indo-European language family, specifically identified with India, although it spread throughout all of South Asia. Pali, an Indo-Aryan language, was also spoken in Cambodia, but it was used primarily for religious purposes.

The foremost Western expert on Cambodian history, David Chandler, said, "Sanskrit inscriptions, in verse, praise the actions of kings and the elite, such as building Hindu temples." Sanskrit was the language and text of the upper classes. It marked the difference between "those who grew rice" and those who did not. When a person mastered Sanskrit, it was said they were "rescued from the mud," meaning they weren't among those who worked in the rice paddies. It was possible to climb the ladder and reach a more elite status, but that didn't happen often.

The Funan Kingdom

The first known polity of Cambodia was the Funan Kingdom. Historians estimate that Funan existed from the 1st century CE to the 6th century CE. The term "Funan" means "Mountain Kingdom" in Khmer. The name was given to this state, which covered the southern tip of the Indochinese Peninsula, by two itinerant Chinese cartographers, who were also traders and diplomats. Funan was described as an "Indianized" state, meaning it was influenced by Indian culture. However, it was more a collection of loose communities rather than a proper state. Those communities were united by religion and the economy, and they depended upon rice as their prime commodity. It isn't known what the people who lived there called themselves or their region, which is why historians use the term "Funan" to refer to them.

Linguists have stated that the language of the people who settled in Funan spoke, for the most part, Mon-Khmer. This is an Austroasiatic language, and it is also the indigenous language of Thailand (called the Kingdom of Siam in the early days) and Myanmar. Since the majority of the people spoke Mon Khmer, scholars believe most of the people were Khmers, although they claim it is possible that Austronesian-speaking peoples might have been present as well. In prehistorical days, the Austronesian people were a seafaring group who populated maritime Southeast Asia, including modern-day Taiwan and Oceania. The Austronesians invented very early sailing vessels like catamarans.

Mythological Foundations

The earliest people of the land believed the sun and moon were deities, much like other cultures around the world. Funan has an ancient legend regarding a foreigner by the name of Huntian. As the story relates, Huntian arrived in the land of Funan and desired a dragon princess. The term "dragon princess" comes from the teachings in one of the Vedic Sanskrit narrations, the *Rig Veda*. As the legend states, Huntian shot a magic arrow into the princess's boat, which reportedly frightened her into marrying him. In exchange, the girl's father "enlarged the possessions of his son-in-law by drinking up the water that covered the country, thus exposing the land." This myth was passed to Cambodia from India.

Some scholars believe Huntian is the same figure as Kaundinya, whose tales are marked in Sanskrit inscriptions. However, there are disputes among scholars about that assignation, as there is a difference in syllables. Huntian is also known by the name Preah Thong in the Khmer culture, the vernacular language of the Cambodians.

According to the Chinese *Book of Liang,* "The people of the Funan kingdom originally had the custom of going naked, tattooing their bodies and letting their hair hang down." As the narration continued, it said that the Funan ruler was a female named Liuye. She is perhaps better known as Queen Soma, the daughter of the king of the Nagas, but she was also known as Neang Neak in Khmer. The "Nagas" are serpent beings in Buddhist mythology. A Hindu brahman, or priest of the gods, named Huntian (Kaundinya) surprised her with his unannounced arrival. As the story goes on,

"Huntian taught Liuye to make a hole in a piece of cloth and put her head through it, using it as clothing to cover her body." Another version relates that Huntian shot an arrow at Liuye's ship when she tried to pillage his vessel. Either way, she gave herself up to him, and they became husband and wife, the first royal couple of Funan.

In the 1ˢᵗ century, Queen Soma and King Kaundinya reigned over Funan. Eventually, the land was segmented into many kingdoms, one of which became today's Cambodia.

The Culture and Lifestyle of Funan

The Funan Kingdom arose in the Mekong Delta on the southern tip of the Indochinese Peninsula, encompassing all of current-day Cambodia, segments of Thailand to the north, and Vietnam to the east. Therefore, Funan covered the strategically important coastline along the South China Sea to the east and the Bay of Thailand and the Bay of Bengal to the west.

A temple in Funan

Two theories have been promulgated about the location of Funan's capital. It may have been near today's town of Banam or possibly a town known as Vyadhapura ("City of the Hunter"). Funan was divided into city-states made up of residential villages.

The people raised rice and root crops, and irrigation and the draining of wet terraces were made more systemic as time went on.

The king's dwelling had "double terraces," with palisades around it instead of walls. The roof was made of algae. Elephants were the kings' primary means of transport. As the people further developed villages, they began to war with each other. Slaves were often taken after these raids.

The lords of these villages felt they needed the divine protection of Shiva, the deity of rebirth. Thus, the people believed in reincarnation. They had ascetic brahmans who wandered the villages, teaching the people about devotion to Shiva and imparted the notions of karma. Karma is based on a person's behavior; a person who performs good acts has a good future, while those who don't suffer the consequences of their negative actions. The goal of Hinduism is a release from one's physical and mental suffering and an end to the repeated cycles of rebirth in the human state.

Sanskrit was the royal language of Funan, while Mon-Khmer was the language the majority of the people spoke. Taxes were paid in gold, silver, perfumed wood, or pearls. The brahmans were educated and had large book collections. Both Hinduism and, to some extent, Buddhism thrived in Funan. The ancient *Book of Liang*, complied by Yao Sillian, indicates that King Rudravarman (6th century CE) requested copies of the texts from the Chinese when traders visited, which serves as proof of Funan's interest in Buddhism.

Funan depended upon trade via the Maritime Silk Road and reached its height during the 3rd century CE under King Fan Shiman. Under him, Funan had a large fleet and a complex bureaucracy based on a tribute system. If a polity, such as Funan, wished to conduct trade with other nations, it would send envoys to those emperors or kings, kowtow to them, and acknowledge their superiority and precedence, who would then grant permission to conduct trade. The Indian Ocean trade routes, sometimes called the "Monsoon Marketplace," connected Funan to India via the Gulf of Siam (current-day Gulf of Thailand), through the Andaman Sea and the Bay of Bengal. In the east, the vessels would move along the Isthmus of Kra in Malay, take a coastland journey along the Gulf of Thailand, and then travel around the Mekong Delta, hugging the coast of Vietnam to reach China. That route, called the Trans-Asiatic route, was an off-shoot of the larger Maritime Silk Road. Exports from Funan were forest products, gold, elephants, rhinoceros' horns, ivory, kingfisher feathers, and spices.

Oc Eo was a Funan port of call. It had a series of vertical and horizontal canals that led to Ta Keo in Cambodia, so it was most likely used as a trade route. Due to the buildup of sediment over the many years, Oc Eo is no longer a port. According to the ancient geographers, it bore the name "Kattigara."

The Maritime Silk Road

https://en.wikipedia.org/wiki/Maritime_Silk_Road#/media/File:Austronesian_mar itime_trade_network_in_the_Indian_Ocean.png

In the lowlands of Funan, the wet monsoon season, which lasted between May and October, brought driving rains to the southwest. The Chinese annals called Funan a "realm wrested from the mud." The people lived in stilt houses and cultivated rice paddies. From

December to April, it was (and still is) the dry monsoon season, which brought sunny and hot weather, especially in January and February.

It was said that Hun Pan-huang was the son of Kaundinya I (Preah Thong or Huntian) and Queen Soma. The fifth ruler (if one includes Queen Soma), Fan Shiman, "had large ships built, and sailing all over the immense sea, he attacked more than ten kingdoms. He extended his territory five or six thousand li [about 1,553 square miles]." Funan reached its peak during Fan Shiman's reign in the early 3rd century CE. He created a feudal society and sent ambassadors to China and India in the interests of trade and diplomacy. The Indianization of Funan most likely occurred during this time.

It is believed that Fan Shiman established a small trade monopoly in the region. The people were rather well-to-do at the time, as they used silver utensils. Taxes were paid in pearls, perfumes, and gold.

The Funan Kingdom ended after Rudravarman's death circa 545 CE. However, some historians dispute this, basing the end of the kingdom on a single remark made in the Chinese annals from the Sui dynasty. According to these historians, Rudravarman was succeeded by Bhavavarman I, whose reign ran until circa 590 CE. It further states that his successor was his brother, Chitrasena, who styled himself as King Mahendravarman. Yet another theory states that Chitrasena and Bhavavarman I together conquered the Funan Kingdom and created the Chenla Kingdom. The ancient inscriptions say that Bhavavarman I conquered Funan "at the tip of a sword."

There are several theories about why Funan collapsed. Some say the Trans-Asiatic sea route was supplanted by trade with the island of Sumatra, which was farther south of Funan. If that was the case, Funan would have needed to establish overland trade in order to dominate the region. Given the competition of these kingdoms, that wouldn't have been an easy undertaking.

Chenla Kingdom – 6ᵗʰ Century to 802 CE

Most historians believe that Bhavavarman I was not a part of the ruling dynasty of Funan. They think he expanded Cambodia after he conquered Funan. However, as mentioned above, this is disputed among scholars. And the disagreements don't end there, as there are claims that Chenla, also known as Zhenla, never existed as a centralized kingdom. Modern historians indicate that Chenla was actually a loose confederation of principalities.

Bhavavarman I followed the tradition of Shaivism, a branch of Hinduism that recognizes the deity, Shiva, as the supreme being. Shiva is seen as the creator and destroyer of life. Shaivism embraces an ascetic form of life and values the practice of yoga as a means to be one with Shiva. Shiva is sometimes represented along with Vishnu, who is considered the preserver of life. In the year 590 CE, Bhavavarman I was succeeded by Chitrasena, who took the name Mahendravarman I. In view of the fact that there were sometimes hostilities among Indochinese countries, Mahendravarman sent an ambassador to the neighboring kingdom of Champa to ensure cordial relations.

The height of the Chenla Kingdom occurred under King Isanavarman, who followed Mahendravarman. Isanavarman ruled over the Chenla Kingdom from 616 to 637 CE. An inscription during his reign states, "The great King Isanavarman is full of glory and bravery. He is the King of Kings, who rules over Suvarnabhumi until the sea, which is the border, while the kings in the neighboring states honor his order to their heads." Isanavarman conquered some principalities in northwestern Cambodia and made his capital Isanapura. A Hindu temple complex called Sambor Prei Kuk is believed to have been Isanapura, and today, it is a UNESCO World Heritage Site, located in Kampong Thom Province. Much of the complex was destroyed during the subsequent wars that ravaged Cambodia, but there were originally 150 temples and sacred buildings at the site.

People were expected to make donations at these sacred places. Those included goods, land, and slaves, which would be given to the king. Taxes were collected at the temples, including minor ones. Since lands were donated, their grounds became larger. It did, however, subtract valuable farmland from the commoners. The temples served to attract more business from foreigners and add to the prestige of the kingdom. The construction of the temples required sandstone, which looks quite elegant but is heavy. Therefore, a lot of slaves were needed to haul it.

Religion

Buddhism, which also originated in India, was practiced in Cambodia as well. Although the people of Cambodia originally observed Hindu, historians conjecture that Buddhism traveled to Cambodia via the traders on the Maritime Silk Road. The two religions coexisted peaceably in the country. Twentieth-century Indian historian Himanshu Prabha Ray indicated that Buddhism was more common among those who partook in the Maritime Silk Road, while Brahmic Hinduism was prevalent among farmers. Deities, such as Brahma, Krishna, Indra, and Lakshmi, were worshiped, and their statuary exists among the ruins of sacred sites.

Shiva (top) and Buddha (bottom)

According to historians, the kings did not enforce Hinduism, Buddhism, or any other religion upon their people.

The Hindus used cremation to dispose of deceased persons. The crematoriums were devoted to the veneration of members of the brahman caste. Even today, people gather at the burial sites of their ancestors during Pitru Paksha, which lasts for two weeks, where they offer prayers to their deceased loved ones, often bringing them sticky rice balls to feed upon. They pray and call upon their ancestors to accept their gifts of food. If their sins are not too big, the ancestors are allowed to eat the food, which they do only after sunset.

Social Status

As elucidated earlier, the most common languages spoken in Cambodia during the 7th century were Sanskrit and Khmer. Sanskrit was the language of religion, and those who became more learned in Sanskrit were sometimes granted higher positions.

Society wasn't divided along gender lines, but it was separated into the rich and the poor. Women often played important roles in religious rituals. Slavery existed, and the children of slaves would become slaves themselves. If one owed a debt and couldn't pay it off, they worked off the debt through slavery, similar to indentured servants.

Economy

The economy was based upon wet-rice agriculture and the mobilization of manpower. An extensive irrigation system was built to provide the proper amount of water to the rice paddies and to control run-off. The kingdom produced surpluses of rice, which they traded. In fact, at the ruins of the former seaport Oc Eo, materials from other countries have been found by archaeologists.

Water and Land Chenla

Jayavarman I ruled Chenla from approximately 657 to 681 CE. Jayavarman left no male heirs, and his daughter, Jayadevi, became the new monarch. Her succession was contested, and many conflicts arose. During her reign, Chenla was split into two: "Water Chenla" and "Land Chenla." Jayadevi deeply lamented these divisions, but she was not able to reunite the kingdom.

Land Chenla referred to the upper region of Cambodia, while Water Chenla was located near the Mekong Delta in the lower area of Cambodia. The two groups split their land based upon the geological features of their territories. The people of Land Chenla reportedly lived a peaceable life, but the people of Water Chenla were subject to attacks from Javanese pirates, who sailed up from their islands that were located south of the Indochinese Peninsula. Java was ruled by the Shailendra dynasty at the time. Shailendra means "King of the Mountain," although the term may have been copied from the Funan people. In the late 8th century, Water Chenla became the vassal of the Shailendra. The last of the Water Chenla kings is believed to have been killed, with his people being incorporated into a polity under the Javanese monarchy, in 790 CE.

There is very little known about Land Chenla, except for the mentions of it during the reign of Jayavarman II. In 802, Jayavarman solidified his kingdom, and he is seen as the founder of the Khmer Empire.

Chapter 2 – Khmer Empire, 802–1150

The Khmer Empire, also known as the Angkor Empire, existed between 802 and 1431. The word "Angkor" is derived from the Sanskrit word *nagara*, meaning city. Most of the knowledge of the Khmer Empire doesn't come from the written records of its own historians. Instead, it is pieced together from stone inscriptions or steles about the kings, archaeological evidence, narrations by Chinese traders and various diplomats, and bas-reliefs depicting market scenes, palace life, military endeavors, and daily life. For example, knowledge about one of Cambodia's capitals, Indrapura, has come from the Sdok Kok Thom inscription in Thailand.

Khmer Language

The Khmers of Cambodia spoke a dialect of the Khmer language. Today, Khmer is the official language of Cambodia, with the vast majority speaking Central Khmer. The Khmer people in sections of Thailand speak Surin Khmer (Northern Khmer), and the Khmer people who live in modern-day Vietnam speak Southern Khmer. The three varieties of the language—Central, Northern, and Southern—are mutually intelligible. David Chandler, the eminent Cambodian historian, said, "Khmer inscriptions are all in prose.

They record the founding of temples and the details of temple administration." Khmer was the language used for everyday purposes, and it was also one of the most commonly spoken vernacular languages in all of Southeast Asia.

Ancient Khmer Script

https://en.wikipedia.org/wiki/Khmer_script#/media/File:AncientKhmerScript.jpg

The Mon Language

The Mon language is an Austroasiatic language spoken in Myanmar (formerly Burma) and Thailand. It is closely related to the Khmer language. Mon is called a "lingua franca," or "bridge language," as it is a dialect that makes it possible for people with different native languages to communicate with each other.

Early Kings of the Khmer Empire

In 802 CE, the great ruler Jayavarman II took over what historians call the Khmer Empire (Jayavarman would have called it Kambuja). At the beginning of his reign, he went to a sacred mountain, Mount **Mahendraparvata**, now known as Phnom Kulen, to declare the kingdom's independence. According to David Chandler, Jayavarman II made himself the "universal monarch" and had the ceremony conducted in such a way that "made it impossible for Java to control holy Cambodia." It is not known for certain whether "Java" refers to the island or Champa, a collection of polities in Vietnam. It is even possible it might be referring to something else entirely. According to some scholars, Jayavarman II originally came from the Shailendra court in Java and brought back the culture from that region. Historians have also conjectured that Jayavarman II began his career in Vyadhapura in eastern Cambodia. Archaeological evidence there indicates that he had some relations with the Chams, who lived in the neighboring province of Champa. Since they were a closer threat than the Shailendra, it is quite plausible that the inscription might refer to Champa.

Jayavarman II widened his territory as his reign progressed, allowing for the king to move his capital to Hariharalaya near Cambodia's modern-day town of Rolous. He conquered various territories, including the city of Vyadhapura, Sambhupura, Banteay Prei Nokor, and possibly Wat Pu, which is in present-day Laos.

Jayavarman II's name shows up in several inscriptions (none of which he made himself), but perhaps the most important is the one at the Sdok Kok Thom temple in Thailand. This inscription was made during the 11th century, which was two centuries after Jayavarman died. The writing speaks of the exploits of the Angkor's founding families and their service to the Khmer court and to the chaplains of the Shaivite Hindu religion.

Jayavarman II died in 835, and his successors continued to expand the kingdom. Sadly, there is not much information on the kings of Cambodia who ruled during the 9th century. Epigraphists have said that the only evidence of the three kings who followed Jayavarman II are the names inscribed on steles found at Preah Ko in Hariharalaya. Researchers, such as the noted Cambodian historian Michael Vickery, reported that the contemporaneous inscriptions are the most trustworthy, but there are doubts about the reliability of inscriptions made after that date, including the names and reigns of successive kings and queens.

It has been written that Jayavarman III, who followed his father, Jayavarman II, hunted elephants, but little else was said about him. Jayavarman III died in 877, with Indravarman I taking the throne. He was notable for his building projects, setting the foundation for future rulers. He built the temple of Preah Ko, which he dedicated to his maternal father and grandfather, as well as Jayavarman II, his uncle. Indravarman had a peaceful rule, which was why he was most likely able to commission so many new buildings.

Indravarman died in 889, and his son, Yasovarman I, took over, ruling from 889 to 900. It was said he had leprosy and that he died of the disease; however, it is hard to discern legend from fact when it comes to centuries-old inscriptions.

Yasovarman, the Leper King

*https://en.wikipedia.org/wiki/Yasovarman_I#/media/
File:Phnom_Bakheng_relief_(2009).jpg*

Yasovarman founded many monasteries, or *ashrams*. These would serve as rest stops for the king on his journeys. He most notably moved the capital to Yasodharapura (Angkor). There are many reasons why he made this move, although it is believed the major reason was the old capital had become too crowded. Here, there was ample space for new religious monuments. Some of the most famous Cambodian structures, such as Angkor Wat, would be built at Yasodharapura, as it would serve as the capital of the Khmer Empire for the next 600 years. Yasovarman also continued with his predecessor's huge water projects. By this time, the country had a centralized state with royal heads appointed to run the various provinces.

There is not much known about the kings who immediately followed Yasovarman I. King Rajendravarman II, who started his reign in 944, was the next notable king. According to inscriptions from during his reign, Rajendravarman was victorious over Ramanya and Champa. Historians indicate that Ramanya might have been a part of modern-day Thailand. The inscriptions stated that Rajendravarman II's sword was often stained with blood, indicating that he was an experienced and fierce warrior.

King Jayavarman V and Women Power

Rajendravarman II passed away in 968, and he was succeeded by his ten-year-old son, Jayavarman V. Since he was so young, he didn't truly rule in the early years of his reign, leaving that to the court officials. Jayavarman was a Shaivite, but he tolerated Buddhism, which had begun to flourish in Southeast Asia by the 9th century. Buddhism teaches tolerance for all, and as a result of these beliefs, Jayavarman awarded many women positions in his administration. The Chinese annals indicated that women in Kambuja were noted for their knowledge of astronomy and politics. After Jayavarman V died in 1001, a turbulent period followed. Three kings reigned simultaneously, constantly warring against each other for the throne.

Suryavarman I

By 1006, Suryavarman I had risen to the throne. It was said that he was not Cambodian by blood but was linked to the Cambodian elite. Historians theorize that he rose to the throne through local warfare and the formation of coalitions. Suryavarman also established diplomatic relations with the Chola dynasty in southern India. That was fortunate, as he enlisted their aid to help him deal with attacks from the Tambralinga kingdom, located on the Malay Peninsula, and its later ally, the Srivijaya Empire. Religious overtones were involved in these wars because Khmer and Chola were Hindu Shaivites, while Tambralinga and the Srivijaya Empire were Mahayana Buddhists. The Khmer and Chola proved victorious in these conflicts.

Suryavarman fought in many skirmishes with his neighbors, but he was shrewd. When he didn't want to war with a kingdom for control, he formed coalitions by virtue of marriages. Suryavarman moved steadily westward, conquering smaller principalities. He won his final battle "from a king surrounded by other kings," according to the inscriptions found on temple steles. One of his early actions was to require his officials to take oaths of loyalty called *tamvrac*. They would swear, "If all of us...do not keep this oath with regard to His Majesty, may he still reign long, we ask that he inflict on us royal punishment of all sorts."

Suryavarman II

Under the weight of its internal conflicts and skirmishes with neighboring kingdoms, the Khmer Empire underwent a weak period of central power. An ambitious prince by the name of Suryavarman claimed rights to the throne. One of the inscriptions stated, "He approved the desire of the royal dignity of his family"; in other words, this inscription claims he had a right to assume the throne. However, Suryavarman had to deal with two opposing claimants, Nripatindravarman and Dharanindravarman I, the latter of whom was his great-uncle. Suryavarman, who was "bounding on the head of the elephant of the enemy king...killed him, as Garuda [mystical bird of prey]...would kill a serpent." It is hard to know to which of the two men this inscription refers, but regardless, Suryavarman II took the throne in 1113.

During the reign of King Suryavarman II, the empire attained its greatest geographic extent, as Suryavarman sought to unify the land under his rule.

Khmer Empire – Dai Viet and Champa (Champa is green)

https://upload.wikimedia.org/wikipedia/commons/4/45/VietnamChampa1.gif

The Dai Viet-Khmer Wars

In 1128, King Suryavarman II demanded tribute payments from Dai Viet, whose current monarch was only about thirteen years old. Dai Viet refused, so Suryavarman decided to exact tribute from them by taking some of their lands, forming an army of 20,000 soldiers in order to do so. He lost the early battles, but he returned with 700 ships the next year. By 1132, Khmer had allied with

Champa, which also saw a way to gain new lands. That year, the Khmer Empire and Champa invaded Dai Viet. In 1136, Dai Viet penetrated into Khmer territory and attacked with 30,000 troops. However, they were forced to retreat. War historians have labeled the outcome of this war as inconclusive, as neither side really gained or lost any lands. In addition, after the two monarchs of the respective kingdoms passed, they were both succeeded by weaker rulers.

The Khmer–Cham Wars

Khmer and Champa had been engaged in conflicts throughout the years, starting back in 950. King Suryavarman II reignited the war in 1145 after the conclusion of the Dai Viet war. After his failure in Dai Viet, Suryavarman II invaded Champa and occupied its capital city, Vijaya. He then destroyed temples at My Son, which was a religious center and the burial site for Champa's royalty.

In the process, Suryavarman II deposed the Cham king, Jaya Indravarman III. The following year, he annexed Champa and put a new king on the throne, who historians believe might have been Suryavarman's brother-in-law. That was short-lived, as the Cham retook the capital and killed the new king. In 1150, Suryavarman tried to take Champa again but was unsuccessful.

Angkor Wat

Suryavarman II initiated the construction of the magnificent temple complex of Angkor Wat. By land area, it is the largest religious monument in the world.

This temple was originally dedicated to the god Vishnu, the preserver of life. Vishnu's role is to return to Earth during times of great need to restore order and peace within the balance of good and evil. The *Rig Veda*, the sacred Hindu text, says, "Through all this world strode Vishnu: thrice his foot he planted, and the whole world was gathered in his footsteps, Vishnu, the Guardian, whom none deceiveth, made three steps and established his laws."

Rice and other produce were stored in the temples throughout the empire for times of need. Maize, rice, and wheat were collected for the benefit of the state, that is, for the people, as well as for the priests and advisors to the kings. The temples were essentially the basis of the economy, as they acted as distribution centers, receiving goods from the villages and then sending them outward into the local villages. Goods were distributed first to those with power and prestige before being given to those in the countryside.

The Story of the Churning of the Ocean of Milk

The *devas* (gods) and the *asuras* (demons) stirred up the cosmic ocean—the Kshirasagara—to obtain the *amrita*, or the elixir of immortality. As they churned the ocean, from the great depths arose a deadly poison called Halahala. The poison obscured their sight and filled the sky with choking smoke. The *devas* and *asuras* appealed to the great Shiva for help. Rushing to help his beloved beings on Earth, he swallowed some of the poison to keep it from spreading. The greedy *devas* and *asuras* rushed to snatch the *amrita* when it appeared, clawing and biting each other for it, but Vishnu, disguised as an enchantress named Mohini, coerced the *asuras* to give the potion to "her." Vishnu gave the *amrita* to the *devas*. Svarbhanu, an *asura*, disguised himself as a *deva* and tried to drink of the *amrita*, the holy nectar. Vishnu decapitated him for this deception.

A bas-relief at Angkor Wat depicts this story, and other stories from Hinduism can be found there as well. This particular relief shows the great ocean being churned by the two *asuras* and *devas*. There is also a depiction of the serpent named Vasuki, who Vishnu used to stir up the great waters.

Angkor Wat, Temple Complex of the Khmer Empire

The Beginning of the Decline

Suryavarman passed away in 1150, perhaps during his campaign against Champa. He was succeeded by Dharanindravarman II, who kicked off a long period of weak rulers.

There were a lot of factors that went into Khmer's demise. For instance, geologists have noted that the water in the area of Angkor Wat was reduced over time and probably became tapped out. The basis of Angkor's rice-based economy depended upon an intricate system of canals and reservoirs. The water provided subsistence for a large population, as there were perhaps as many as 600,000 at Angkor Wat and the surrounding areas alone. The Angkor Wat area reached its height of efficiency during the mid-12th century and started to shrink during the following century.

Lack of maintenance factored into the decline of the empire as well, which was due to the labor shortage during times of war. Weak rulers, civil wars, and the shift from Hinduism to Buddhism also played a role.

Chapter 3 – The Khmer Empire and the Later Khmer Kingdom, 1150–1600

Not much was written about the immediate successors of Suryavarman. Dharanindravarman II, who was possibly Suryavarman's cousin, took the throne in 1150, and he was followed by Yasovarman II in 1160. According to an inscription, Yasovarman II put down a revolt in the northwest by people who were neither foreigners nor members of the elite; they were depicted as people with "animal heads" in bas-reliefs at the temple of Banteay Chhmar. In 1167, Yasovarman II was assassinated by one of his subordinates, who then seized the throne. That man was Tribhuvanaditya, and he held the throne until 1177.

Sack of Angkor

The rebellions in the Khmer Empire provided Champa with an opportunity to invade them. In 1170, the Chams attacked, but the outcome of the war was inconclusive. The king of Champa, Jaya Indravarman IV, and his troops tried again in 1177, this time taking the current capital, Yasodharapura (Angkor), and slaughtering Tribhuvanaditya.

A courageous Khmer by the name of Jayavarman rose to defend his country and led a formidable army against the Chams in 1178. After he ousted the Cham invaders, he returned to the capital and found it in chaos and disorder. Jayavarman discovered that the Khmers were embroiled in their own disputes with each, and he put an end to them by 1181. Once that was accomplished, he crowned himself king.

King Jayavarman VII

Jayavarman VII is considered to be one of Cambodia's greatest kings. He wasn't a legitimate successor to the throne, but he played the part well, as he was very grandiose. Jayavarman VII was a Mahayana Buddhist, which espouses the belief that each person is responsible for his or her own behavior. He was under the impression that he should save his people from suffering. In addition, he tried to integrate Buddhism with the Cambodian ideals of kingship, similar to that of the Hindu monarchs who preceded him.

Since Angkor had been destroyed by the Chams, Jayavarman established a new capital, which he called Angkor Thom. There, he built a magnificent Buddhist temple called the Bayon. There are 216 gigantic faces on the temple, one of whom scholars theorize is of Jayavarman himself. They believe the other faces are of the bodhisattva, who are devout students of Buddha. During its height, Angkor Thom was said to have housed a population of 80,000 to 150,000 people.

The wars between Champa and Cambodia continued for twenty-two more years. In 1203, Jayavarman VII conquered Champa and sacked it. Champa then became a vassal state of the Khmer Empire.

Beware! They May Bite!

Currently, Angkor Thom has been inflicted with macaque monkeys, which have made the temple their home. Part of the reason for this nuisance was the gradual domestication of the monkeys. To this day, tourists adore seeing them, even though the monkeys will snatch food right out of their hands or even attack people. According to *The Phnom Penh Post*, "These monkeys are no longer afraid of people because people have been feeding them. Now when they don't feed them, the monkeys get upset and steal the food anyway and even bite people." In late 2020, the Cambodian government removed some of the monkeys from the temple complex, but it is almost a certainty that there are still some hanging around.

The Bayon, Angkor Thom

https://en.wikipedia.org/wiki/Khmer_Empire#/media/
File:Bayon_(4184833523).jpg

Ancient Cambodian Medicine

Jayavarman VII not only established a network of roads, including way bridges and rest houses for travelers, but he also endorsed the construction of hospitals. It is written that he "suffered from the illnesses of his subjects more than from his own; the pain that affected men's bodies was for him a spiritual pain, and thus more piercing." Therefore, as part of his grand building projects, he included plans for many hospitals, with Ta Prohm Kel perhaps being the most well-known. The inscription at Ta Prohm Kel records the king's oath: "All the beings who are plunged in the ocean of existence, may I draw them out by virtue of this good work." To future generations, the king added, "May the kings of Cambodia who come after me, attached to goodness...attain with their wives, dignitaries, and friends the place of deliverance where there is no more illness."

Traditional Khmer medicine was a combination of traditional Indian medicine called Ayurveda and ancient Chinese medicine. Archaeologists have noted that these hospitals had a division of labor and included hospital managers, drug grinders, drug distributors, and staff to boil water.

Their medicinal practices were recorded on palm-leaf manuscripts, and although some were inevitably destroyed in conflicts, some have survived to this day. Traditional medicines consisted of plant roots, bark, and leaves, with these medicinal properties being mixed in water. Before administering medication, the staff would pour the mixture over a "Shiva Linga." It represented the assistance of Shiva, who would bring health to the patient.

The *kru pet* were the most educated. The *kru thnam* were herbalists, and the *thmup* were sorcerers. These classes are still around today, but there are only a handful of those belonging to the *kru pet* class. There were a variety of other roles, including bonesetters, diviners, and those who created good luck or love charms. Buddhist monks also played a role, especially if an exorcism was needed.

Ta Prohm Kel - An Early Cambodian Hospital

https://en.wikipedia.org/wiki/Traditional_Cambodian_medicine#/media/ File:Ta_Prohm_Kel4.JPG

Society

The Khmer Empire had a similar caste system as the Hindus. The commoners were toward the bottom, while the kshatriya—the nobles and warriors—were at the top. There were other classes, such as the brahmans (priests) and merchants. The slaves, as one might predict, were at the very bottom. The slaves were usually prisoners captured from wars.

Khmer kings were influenced by the cult of Devaraja, a popular concept in Southeast Asia that promoted the idea that kings were divinely chosen to rule. There were many who supported the king, such as his ministers, servants, and guards. However, most of society was a part of the farming community.

Slaves

The slaves were separated into fourteen categories according to their ethnic origin and duties. Some slaves served as musicians and dancers. Those slaves that serviced temples had a higher status, and they enjoyed a semi-clerical status. All of these people could be bought or sold and given away, as they had no freedom. It appears that many slaves were attached to a place, like a farm, for example, as opposed to being attached to a particular lord.

In addition, there were people who entered servitude to work off a debt. Sometimes parents, due to unfortunate economic hardships, were forced to make their children enter bondage slavery.

Farmers

Farmers dwelled in villages near the rice paddies. Their homes had walls made of bamboo, with thatched roofs. Their houses were on stilts to protect them and their belongings from floods during the monsoon season. According to the book by the Chinese historian and diplomat Zhou Daguan, written in the late 13th century, "the dwellings of the princes and principal officials have a completely different layout and dimensions from those of the people...The official rank of each person determines the size of the houses." Nobles had homes with walls made of bamboo, but their roofs were composed of wooden shingles. Of course, they were also much more elaborate than a common farmer.

Farmers were somewhat free in terms of their livelihood. While they were free to grow rice or vegetables, they weren't free to move elsewhere, as rice paddies were designated for particular farmers.

Farmers and free peasants would be called upon to serve in the military. In addition, they were expected to help with public works projects, such as canal building or other favors their lords might ask. They might also be called upon to help at temples during the holy festivals or to clean or refurbish statues.

<u>Clothing</u>

The people wore a sampot, a rectangular cloth worn on the lower body. It was wrapped between the legs and secured with a belt at the back. The material would be simple for the peasants, but the upper classes wore elaborately decorated sampots. Men and women also wore a krama, which has a variety of uses, such as a scarf or bandanna. It can even be used as a hammock for small children.

The Khmers originated the belief that a person's soul resided in their heads, which is something Cambodians still practice to this day. Thus, it is taboo to touch or point with one's feet, especially toward another person. The feet are the lowest part of the body and are thought to be impure, making such a gesture an insult.

Events of the 13th Century

Jayavarman VII died in 1218 and was succeeded by his son, Indravarman II. Like his father, Indravarman II was a Mahayana Buddhist. However, unlike his father, he wasn't skilled in military matters, and he lost control of some of the Champa territories, thus shrinking the size of Kambuja (Cambodia). In 1238, subjects within his kingdom rebelled under Si Inthrathit. He established his own kingdom, which was rather short-lived, as it ended in 1270. Si Inthrathit is often regarded as the ruler who freed Siam (modern-day Thailand) from Cambodian rule.

Indravarman II died in 1243 and was succeeded by Jayavarman VIII. Jayavarman, unlike his predecessors, was a follower of Shaivism. Jayavarman VIII aggressively opposed Buddhism and converted many Buddhist temples to Hindu ones. He systematically went on a destructive spree, defacing Buddhist images and destroying statues.

Between the 1270s and the 1290s, Kublai Khan of the massive Yuan Empire in China engaged in a military campaign in Southeast Asia, attacking kingdoms such as Burma, Vietnam, and Java. Burma was the only spot where the Mongols had any success, but many states agreed to pay tribute to avoid bloodshed. Kublai Khan even threatened the stability of Cambodia, attacking the Khmer Empire in 1283. In exchange for peace, Jayavarman VIII paid Kublai Khan tribute, which included elephant tusks, gold, and other precious items.

Jayavarman VIII was deposed by his son-in-law, Indravarman III, in 1295. King Indravarman III reigned from 1295 until 1308. The wandering Chinese diplomat Zhou Daguan, from whom we get much information about the Khmer Empire, related a curious story about Indravarman. Zhou says that when his father-in-law, Jayavarman VIII, had died, Indravarman III's wife stole his gold sword and gave it to Indravarman. It was said that was the reason why Jayavarman VIII's own son didn't succeed to the throne. Zhou also embroidered on the legend, saying, "The new king had a sacred piece of iron embedded in his body, so that if anything like a knife or an arrow touched him, he could not be injured."

Indravarman's procession when he became king was like those of the older days—replete in magnificence and glory and drawing great crowds. According to Zhou's accounts:

Each time he came out, all his soldiers were gathered in front of him, with people bearing banners, musicians and drummers following behind him. One contingent was made up of three to five hundred women of the palace. They wore clothes with a floral design and flowers in their coiled-up hair, and carried huge candles, alight even though it was daylight...All the ministers, officials and relatives of the king were in front, riding elephants...Late came the king, standing on an elephant, the gold sword in his hand and the trunks of his elephant encased in gold.

Cambodia shifted away from the intolerance of his predecessor, Jayavarman VIII. Indravarman III followed Theravada Buddhism, which he made the state religion. Theravada Buddhism promotes more conservative beliefs. The focus is placed upon doctrine, rules of behavior, and the discourses and sermons of the Buddha.

Followers are expected to meditate daily in order to free themselves from the attachments of the flesh, as that is the path to enlightenment.

The Theravada monks looked different too. According to Zhou Daguan's description in his book, *Customs of Cambodia*, he said that Theravada monks "shave their heads and dress in yellow. They leave their right shoulder uncovered, and wrap themselves in a robe made of yellow cloth and go barefoot." People were expected to support the monks by providing food, supplies, and medicine to them.

Local Marketing

Zhou Daguan presented a detailed description of the rural marketing practices in Cambodia, and historians have noted that they weren't much unlike Cambodian markets today. Zhou said that it was mostly conducted by women. The markets were open from early in the morning until mid-day. They didn't have stalls; instead, they simply unrolled mats on the ground. Like today's local markets, Zhou speculated that fees were charged to rent each space. They sold ivory, rhinoceros' horns for lowering fevers, lacquer, beeswax, and cardamom. Imported goods were also sold and consisted of metal goods, silk, porcelain, paper, and wicker.

The Decline of Khmer

Numerous factors fed into the decline of the Khmer Empire, which began its downfall slowly over the 13th century. The state's conversion from Hinduism to Mahayana Buddhism to Theravada Buddhism changed social and government systems. Over time, kings and the Hindu priests (brahmans) began to diminish in terms of importance; for example, kings lost their standing as being divinely chosen. Therefore, there was no need to erect more shrines, statues, or temples in their honor. The change in ideology also contributed to the lack of attention to infrastructure. Throughout the years, the Cambodian water management system began to fall into disrepair, as it hadn't been maintained. Therefore, floods and droughts were frequent, leading to crop failures.

The last Khmer king to have been mentioned in the monument inscriptions was Jayavarman IX, whose reign started in 1327, but others succeeded him, as the Khmer Empire didn't end until 1431. Jayavarman was a devoted Hindu, and he was assassinated in 1336 by the head of the royal gardens, whom historians assume took the throne, although it is very likely this story is simply legend and not fact.

Foreign Relations

Between 1371 and 1432, twenty-one tributary missions were sent from Cambodia to the Ming court. This wasn't the first time missions had been sent to China from Khmer, but this number eclipsed those from previous years. The Cambodians were most eager to expand and exploit trade relations but were hampered by competition with the up-and-coming Ayutthaya Kingdom, which was centered in modern-day Thailand.

Around 1352, the Ayutthaya Kingdom invaded Khmer and replaced their rulers with Siamese kings. In 1357, Suryavamsa Rajadhiraja regained his throne, but he lost it again in 1393. When the Siam king, who also ruled the Khmer Empire, was assassinated, Ponhea Yat took his rightful place on the throne in Angkor.

However, Angkor was no longer a powerful city. The war with Ayutthaya had devastated the region. And not only that, but the government had failed to maintain the Cambodian hydraulic systems around Angkor. There are many other theories regarding the fall of Angkor, such as natural disasters, disease, and the decline of the royal cult. It is possible many of these factors played a role. Regardless, in 1431, Ponhea Yat moved the capital of Cambodia to the city of Phnom Penh. At Phnom Penh, the confluence of the Mekong River, the Tonle Sap, and the Bassac River served to stimulate trade. Phnom Penh was a fortified city, which allowed vigorous trade to occur. Pottery, fish, and fish sauce were exchanged for Chinese goods.

Around this time, a legend arose regarding the importance of Phnom Penh to explain this shift of control. It was said that an old woman discovered a Buddha image miraculously floating downstream to Phnom Penh. Historians consider the move to Phnom Penh the end of the Khmer Empire. It was replaced by a rather weak Khmer kingdom.

The Longvek Era

Ang Chan was perhaps the best-known post-Angkor king. He was the viceroy and heir apparent of Phnom Penh, and in 1512, he came into conflict with a man named Sdach Korn. Sdach Korn killed the reigning king and drove Ang Chan out of the capital. Ang Chan fled to Siam and returned with a Siamese army in 1516, determined to expel the pretender. Sdach Korn retreated, and Ang took his rightful place on the throne. However, Sdach had not given his crown up, as he continued to label himself as the king. Fortunately, Ang was able to obtain firearms and cannons during the civil war. Around 1528 (possibly 1529), he captured Sdach Korn and beheaded him. That same year, he established the capital in the city of Longvek, which was on the banks of the Tonle Sap.

Ang Chan, who would rule until 1566, most likely made this move for a number of reasons. One of the major reasons was the devastation of the Khmer territory over the years. The Kingdom of Siam had made many incursions throughout the 14th century, and moving the capital to Longvek was smart military-wise, as it had a more defensible terrain. In addition, Longvek was located on the banks of the Tonle Sap, giving the Cambodians at least some limited access to trade networks. The historians of the time said, "Even though they appeared to have a secondary role in the Asian commercial sphere in the 16th century, the Cambodian ports did indeed thrive." Cambodians traded metals, silk, ivory, incense, and the like. The tributaries that were still accessible provided trading opportunities with the Chinese, Arabs, Indonesians, and Malays. Not only were those markets now open, but Europeans also traveled to the area, coming from Spain, the Netherlands, England, and Portugal.

The *Cambodian Royal Chronicles* and the *Royal Chronicles of Ayutthaya* record the numerous military clashes between the two nations, but modern historians, such as David Chandler and Michael Vickery, doubt the accuracy of these documents. What's more, Chandler states that the "least-recorded period of Cambodian history falls between Zhou Daguan's visit to Angkor [at the end of the 13th century] and the restoration of some of the temples there by a Cambodian king named Chan in the 1550s and 1560s." This is why historians refer to this period, particularly between the 15th and 16th centuries, as Cambodia's "Dark Age," as there is little information about the history of Cambodia available. Although sources become a bit more frequent after the 16th century, there still isn't enough to get a full picture of the rulers and their reigns. This lasts up until 1863, which was the beginning of the French protectorate of Cambodia.

Ecological/Epidemiological Threats

During the Longvek era, the Khmer Empire was in decline. Archaeologists have noted multiple reasons why records were sparse, including the ever-present skirmishes, both from within and from without. Other reasons we haven't touched much upon were severe ecological disasters and the black plague.

Scientists theorized that the Black Death first appeared in Cambodia between 1330 and 1345, and the disease was most likely present for a time, with cases popping up even after the first major influx. Besides the Black Death, the excessive waters in the region traditionally give rise to malaria. This would more easily spread due to the poor water management system, as they weren't maintained, and stagnant water causes an increase in malaria-ridden mosquitoes.

When the population of the Khmer kingdom increased, a great strain was placed on the irrigation system, which was compounded by severe droughts alternated with excessive flooding. In addition, the people cut down more trees to create new rice paddies. Without the trees to absorb rainwater, the runoff carried silt downhill, filling up the canals the people used for transportation.

The Continued Rise of the Ayutthaya Kingdom

As the Khmers declined, the Ayutthaya Kingdom (modern-day Thailand) expanded and became a major power in Southeast Asia. In 1568, the Siamese attacked Burma, seeking to annex their lands. However, Burma was victorious, and Ayutthaya became a vassal state. Ayutthaya attempted several times to free itself from Burmese vassalage, but it wouldn't be successful until 1584. Naresuan, one of Thailand's most beloved monarchs, participated in the battle for independence, becoming king in 1590 and ushering in a new age of expansion, one that put Cambodia in its crosshairs

Legend of the Siamese-Cambodian War

Much of history is told in stories and legends, and Cambodia has a rather interesting one about the war with Ayutthaya. It tells the story of two brothers, Preah Ko and Preah Keo. Preah Ko, an ox who was birthed by a human mother, had divine powers and carried precious items in his belly.

As the legend relates, the king of Siam challenges the king of Cambodia, with Preah Ko involving himself to aid his king. The king of Siam is angered by this and sends an army to capture the two brothers. They flee to Longvek ("Lovek" in some records), where they hide in a thick bamboo forest. As the story goes, the king of Siam orders his men to fire silver coins into the bamboo forest. The local people rush in to snatch up the coins, obliterating the forest in the process. The brothers manage to flee once more, but in the end, the king of Siam captures them.

The forest in the legend relates to the Ranam forest, which played a part in the Siamese-Cambodian War.

The Siamese-Cambodian War

In 1591, under General Phra Ratcha Manoo, Siam invaded Cambodia. King Satha I of Cambodia and his men were initially successful at the Ranam forest. However, Siamese reinforcements arrived, pushing the Cambodians out. Soon after, the Longvek citadel was besieged, but after three months, the Siamese were compelled to retreat.

In 1593, King Naresuan of Ayutthaya prepared a fresh assault on Cambodia after dealing with Burma. He divided his forces into four, and they all met to take down Longvek. By January 1594, the armies had met up, and they stormed the city. King Satha fled to Laos, but most of the Cambodian royal family were held as hostages and relocated to Siam (the Ayutthaya Kingdom). While there, they were kept under Siamese influence and control.

The Cambodian-Spanish War

The Spanish had been on decent terms with King Satha I. However, despite the friendly overtures, they couldn't pass up the opportunity to expand their reach. Spain was very invested in spreading Christianity in Southeast Asia, and by gaining the stronghold of Cambodia, they would have an excellent launching-off point to do so. In 1593, Spain sent out an expedition to place a king on the throne who would align with their interests. Although they didn't prevail in the long run, they were able to establish a new king, Ponhea Ton, in 1597. He granted the Spanish the rights to two provinces on the east and west sides of the Mekong River.

Unfortunately, the Spanish were used to more brutal methods to spread Christianity, and Spanish, Portuguese, and Filipino fighters brutally attacked some Malay residences in the area. The Chams, Muslim Malays, and Cambodians retaliated to this move by massacring the Spanish, Portuguese, and Filipinos.

By 1599, Cambodia came under the control of the Ayutthaya Kingdom.

New Capital

The capital of Cambodia moved several times during the post-Angkor period. Besides the already mentioned moves, later ones came during the 1590s and early 1600s, after the Siamese had made their move on Longvek. In the end, the capital was moved to Oudong.

Cambodia (Khmer Kingdom) 1650

Chapter 4 – Colonial Period

Between the 17th and 18th centuries, Cambodia suffered a decline in its economy, as it had lost much of its coastland. Chinese traders, for the most part, bypassed them. By then, their main products to trade were brown sugar of poor quality, lacquer, and deer hides. One of those traders wrote, "Cambodia is a poor country with a poorly organized government and armed forces. There are no rich people."

To maintain a balance of power to contain the Siamese, whose power base was spreading, the king of Cambodia, Chey Chettha II (r. 1618-1628), married into the Nguyen family of Vietnam. He granted the Vietnamese settlements in Prey Nokor (modern-day Ho Chi Minh City). They established a customs house in Prey Nokor, which they used for trading purposes and to collect taxes. That was the start of a wave of Vietnamese immigrants into Cambodia. By the 1690s, Cambodia, which had never really recovered from its war with Ayutthaya, was forced to give the Mekong Delta area to Vietnam. In 1620, the Dutch East India Company also established relations with Cambodia, building an outpost at Kompong Luong, a port near Oudong, three years later.

The Vietnamese and Thai People in Cambodia

In 1636, the more powerful members of the Nguyen dynasty of southern Vietnam split off from the Nguyen overlords in northern Vietnam, annexing areas in the southern Indochinese Peninsula. That cut off Cambodia's southern access to the sea and the Mekong River, affecting their trade. To exacerbate matters, many of the Cambodian ports along the Gulf of Siam were occupied by Sino-Vietnamese troops and private Vietnamese entrepreneurs. Cambodians who lived within those areas were cut off from the rest of Cambodia. That aroused a lot of resentment and anti-Vietnamese feelings. Additionally, it caused a lot of the elite and royal Cambodians who lived there to polarize along pro-Thai and pro-Vietnamese lines. It affected support for the candidates for Cambodian kingship, as their followers would choose kings based upon their support of either Siam or Vietnam.

The severe weakening of Cambodia left a power vacuum in the Mekong Delta. Thus, the Kingdom of Siam (modern-day Thailand) engaged in a power struggle with the Rattanakosin Kingdom of Dai Viet (modern-day Vietnam). The Cambodian kings became puppet kings of the two kingdoms, with a number of conflicts occurring on Cambodian soil. For instance, in 1717, Siam invaded Cambodia to help a sympathetic king regain the throne. Ultimately, Siam won, as the Vietnamese-aligned king switched sides, causing Vietnam to lose the suzerainty of Cambodia.

This polarization tended to weaken the Cambodian royalty in terms of focusing its attention on threats from foreign nations. As a result, in the 1750 and 1760s, there were a series of coups and countercoups by royal rivals.

In 1767, the Kingdom of Ayutthaya was conquered by Burma. A Thai overlord named Taksin set up his own kingdom. He wanted Cambodia to pay him tribute, which they rejected, insulting his honor in the process. King Outey II of Cambodia called Taksin the "son of a Chinese merchant and a commoner." In 1769, partly to uphold his honor and partly to put a new king on the throne, Taksin invaded Cambodia. While he managed to put Ang Non II on the throne, his efforts largely failed.

In 1772, the Tay Son rebellion broke out in Vietnam. This was led by the Tay Son brothers: Nguyen Hue, Nguyen Nhac, and Nguyen Lu. The Siamese sensed an opportunity and decided to push their way into the struggling country. On their way, the Siamese marched through Angkor and sent their navy out on several expeditions, destroying several small ports along the Gulf of Siam. They even burned down Phnom Penh. Just seven years later, the Thai placed seven-year-old Prince Ang Eng on the Cambodian throne under the regency of a pro-Thai official.

In 1782, Taksin was deposed and replaced by the Siamese minister of war, who was campaigning in Cambodia. That same year, Ang Eng had to flee to Siam due to Cham invasions. There was no immediate successor to the throne. Instead, a Cambodian official, Phraya Yommarat (Baen), became the regent, working closely with Siam in the process.

Ang Eng was adopted by Rama I, the Siamese minister of war who took over after Taksin. Eventually, Ang Eng would move back to Cambodia, taking the throne again in 1794. However, not everyone was happy with this move, as they enjoyed Baen as king. To prevent a civil war from breaking out, Rama I ordered Baen to leave Oudong, giving him the governorship of Battambang and Siem Reap instead. In 1796, Ang Eng died, and his five-year-old son, Ang Chan II, succeeded him.

The Culture of 17ᵗʰ- & 18ᵗʰ-Century Cambodia: Study of the *Ramayana*

The Cambodians had seen much grief, but they kept their heritage and legacy alive despite the many wars.

The *Ramayana* is an old Sanskrit epic, cherished and performed in dance by the Cambodians. It was an escape and an inspiration to them; it was a means by which they kept their heritage alive. It is shared by the people of Thailand, Malaysia, Sri Lanka, and other Southeast Asian countries. Little is known about its author, Valmiki. The epic was written in India and describes the concept of a god who has taken a human form. The hero, Rama, must fight to win back his love, Sita, who was kidnapped by a demon.

Throughout the poem, Rama's virtues and strengths are extolled, and he is portrayed as being a model for rightful living. The quotes from *Ramayana* serve to inspire its readers with courage and love. For example, Rama says, "We have no right to ask when a sorrow comes, 'Why did this happen to me?' unless we ask the same question for every joy that comes our way."

Rama with Sita and his brother, Lakshmana, in the forest

The Shy King

Although Ang Chan II was the king of Cambodia, he wasn't allowed to enter the country until he came of age in 1806, remaining in Siam in the meantime. He had to struggle against his two brothers, Ang Em and Ang Snguon, and was forced to pay tribute to Vietnam as well. The Siamese demanded that Ang Chan appoint his two brothers as co-regents or viceroys, but Ang Chan refused. In 1811, with the help of the Siamese, Ang Snguon overthrew his brother and took the throne. Ang Chan fled to Vietnam, and in 1813, the Vietnamese returned to put him back in power, capturing the capital city of Oudong in the process. Ang Em and Ang Snguon fled to Bangkok. Ang Chan II then built two castles for himself—one at Phnom Penh and another at Lvea Aem— the latter of which stationed the bulk of his army. One thousand soldiers were assigned to protect King Ang Chan in Phnom Penh.

During his second reign, Cambodia was a vassal state of Vietnam and Siam. Emperor Gia Long of Vietnam said, "Cambodia is a small country, and we should maintain it as a child. We will be its mother, its father will be Siam."

It seems that Ang Chan II was rarely quoted, and none of his writings have survived. He was, in essence, an actor without lines. Ang Chan was timid, which would account for his silence in the annals. It was said of him that "a fresh wind or the cry of a bird could make him flee." A Vietnamese text states that Ang Chan was ill much of the time, which also might explain his silence.

The Siamese-Vietnamese War of 1831–1834

Cambodia was stuck between two great forces: Thailand and Vietnam. And although things had remained somewhat civil, that situation couldn't last forever. Cambodia had control of the Mekong Delta, which granted it the commerce that ensued from maritime trade. In 1832, under General Bodindecha, the Siamese attempted to conquer the southern area of Vietnam, along with Cambodia as well. The Cambodian king fled the capital, heading toward Vietnam for safety. For the Siamese troops to reach the capital of Vietnam, they had to proceed along the Bassac River toward the Mekong Delta. At the Vam Nao Canal, located between the Hau and the Tien Rivers, the Siamese and Vietnamese fleets met in early 1833. Initially, the Siamese ships prevailed, but the Vietnamese launched a massive counterattack on land. Bodindecha then disembarked his troops. The Siamese soon retreated, as did the Vietnamese.

The Siamese then moved toward the Vinh Te Canal. However, it was too shallow there, so they tried to have the galleys hauled by elephants to Kampot, a city in Cambodia. However, the Cambodian locals revolted and killed the elephant handlers, taking the elephants for themselves and pulling back. In the meantime, the Vietnamese kept attacking the Siamese forces. General Bodindecha told the two Cambodian princes, Ang Em and Ang Snguon, to burn Phnom Penh and take the inhabitants to the city of Battambang. However, the Cambodians rebelled, forcing the Siamese and the two princes to retreat to Siam.

The Siamese attempted again to take over the Cambodian communities controlled by the Vietnamese. Unfortunately for them, they lost, although Battambang remained under the control of Siam. At the end of the war, the Cambodian countryside was devastated, and the Vietnamese controlled most of territorial Cambodia.

Royal Succession

Because the Cambodians had been able to preserve their culture, Emperor Minh Mang of Vietnam appointed General Truong Minh Giang to "Vietnamize" Cambodia. Vietnam wanted the Cambodians to serve in the Vietnamese military, and they also wanted to "reform" their habits, which they considered barbaric. The emperor said, "The barbarians [Cambodians] have become my children now...The people have no knowledge of [advanced] agriculture, using picks and hoes, rather than oxen. They grow enough rice for two meals a day, but they don't store any surplus."

The Vietnamese complained that the Cambodians wore robes without slits up the sides and ate with their fingers. However, the Cambodians resented these policies, and there were minor revolts against the Vietnamese, which began to break out in 1836 and occurred off and on through the years.

In 1835, Queen Ang Mey succeeded the throne. She wasn't the eldest daughter of Ang Chan, but she was preferred by the Vietnamese who installed her. In 1840, her older sister, Princess Baen, attempted to escape to Battambang. She was arrested, along with Queen Ang Mey and their other sisters, and they were later deported to Vietnam. Princess Baen was drowned, possibly being tortured beforehand. Unrest ensued, not just because of her death but also because their queen had been removed. According to one Vietnamese report, "The rebels have established posts along the riverbanks at strategic points. They appear and disappear at will. If our troops look to the east, the rebels escape to the west...They concentrate their forces where the jungle is thick, and in swampy areas where our troops cannot maneuver." Siam snatched the opportunity to invade Cambodia and install a puppet ruler. To help counter the rebellion so they could focus their efforts on Siam, Vietnam reinstated Queen Mey for a brief time. However, Ang Duong claimed he had the right to the throne, and since he was backed by Siam, he posed a great threat to Ang Mey. He was the son of the former king, Ang Eng, who ruled in the late 18th century.

The Siamese-Vietnamese War of 1841–1845

Prince Ang Duong supported Siam against Vietnam as the two countries sought to establish dominance over Cambodia. The military campaigns started when General Bodindecha, who had led the Siamese in the previous war, lay siege to Pursat, a Cambodian community controlled by Vietnam. He was able to establish a peaceful surrender there. Soon after, Emperor Minh Mang of Vietnam had a fatal accident, and the new Vietnamese emperor, Thieu Tri, decided to order a retreat instead of engaging the

Siamese. He had his forces retreat to An Giang Province in the Mekong Delta by that October. In the meantime, Vietnam had taken Cambodian Prince Ang Em to rally the Cambodians for the Vietnamese cause. However, the Siamese aided Ang Duong in gaining the throne, killing those Vietnamese they came across while doing so. The Siamese continued to establish their control and remove Vietnamese influence throughout the rest of 1841.

Between 1842 and 1843, disease and famine raged throughout Cambodia, and the fighting essentially ceased during that time. Cambodia was badly damaged due to these conflicts, and they began to argue amongst themselves, saying that they should switch sides and align with Vietnam. In 1845, Ang Duong had the Vietnamese sympathizers executed. After this, the armies began to make major moves again. A Vietnamese offensive occurred, forcing Bodindecha to march and defend Oudong. After the Siamese and Vietnamese engaged in minor battles to the north and south of Oudong, they decided to negotiate.

It took Ang Duong a bit of time to come around to accepting Vietnamese suzerainty, but he eventually did, allowing an agreement to be reached in 1847. This agreement gave both Siam and Vietnam joint domination over Cambodia, and Ang Duong had to send tribute to both Vietnam and Siam.

The French Protectorate

Cambodia was at peace during the rest of King Ang Duong's reign, but it was a tenuous one. Ang Duong secretly yearned for a future in which the Cambodian people would no longer be involved in these wars. Cambodia needed a stronger power, one who could keep their perennial enemies at bay. Therefore, Ang negotiated with Emperor Napoleon III to get French protection for his country. His successor, King Norodom Prohmbarirak, followed up with the French. In 1862, France established a colony in Cochinchina (modern-day Vietnam), and the governor of Cochinchina realized that in order to expand their power, they needed Cambodia, which helped push the negotiations along. In 1863, France established Cambodia as a protectorate, allowing the monarchy to remain but taking most of the power (such as trade and foreign relations) for itself. Phnom Penh was the center of power, becoming the capital of Cambodia in 1866.

Under the treaty King Norodom signed, France agreed to offer Cambodia protection in exchange for timber concessions and mineral exploration rights. King Norodom was permitted to remain at the royal residence of Phnom Penh, but power was mostly invested in the hands of the French governor-general. In time, Siam agreed to this move, as it was granted the continued control of the city of Angkor and the new control over the province of Battambang. In 1887, since Cambodia was a part of the greater French Indochina, the governor-general ruled from the city of Saigon and later moved to Hanoi, which are both located in Vietnam. A resident-general was also appointed, and he was assisted by the local governors in Cambodia. Occasional revolts broke out against the king's acquiescence to French rule, but they were put down quickly by the French government.

The French also wanted Norodom to help pay the costs of the French protectorate through taxes on the sale of opium and liquor. In the 1880s, the French tightened their control on the Cambodian court, as they wanted Cambodia to change some of its traditional customs and to gain a firmer grip on its economy, but the Cambodians resisted.

Norodom assigned his son, also named Norodom, to be his heir apparent. However, he got into a disagreement with the French, and when King Norodom passed in 1904, the throne went to his half-brother, Sisowath, instead. Sisowath supported the French, and they paid him in kind, building him a new palace and granting him a huge ration of opium each year.

Since the French brought in reforms, such as reducing the king's powers and the abolition of slavery, the king became a mere figurehead.

Cambodian Revolt

Not every Cambodian agreed with these French actions, as they saw the French as invading and imposing their own ideas onto them. In 1885, before Norodom's death, some Cambodians revolted under Norodom's other half-brother, Si Votha. The French refused to help initially, as they saw this as perfect leverage to get Norodom to sign new reforms. Eventually, Norodom signed, and the French helped quell the rebellion.

Reorganization of the Government

In 1896, Great Britain, which controlled nearby Burma and British Malay, and France signed a sphere of influence agreement regarding the Indochinese Peninsula, especially the Kingdom of Siam. Under that agreement, Siam ceded Battambang back to Cambodia.

Although the Cambodian sovereignty itself was left intact, the French gained even more control. Cambodia was considered a revenue-producing country. However, corruption was rampant, and banditry was common. Although the Cambodians paid high taxes, the tax rolls were misrepresented, and rice harvests were underestimated. French officials were paid high salaries while the people had trouble making ends meet. Of course, this only added to the resentment Cambodians felt toward the French.

Economy

Cambodia paid higher taxes than the other French Southeast Asian colonies. Their economy was built on rice and peppers. When French investors came in, they created an automobile industry. Minority groups handled industrial and commercial work. Some were immigrants from Champa. The Kui (or Kuy) people from modern-day Thailand and Laos smelted iron ore in the north.

Rural trade was operated by the barter system, and an important railway was built, connecting Phnom Penh and Battambang on the Siamese border.

Under the French, more modern agricultural techniques were introduced, and colonial entrepreneurs were granted concessions in Battambang Province. Cotton and corn were also raised. Rubber plantations were established and headed by French investors. However, the jobs at those plantations were given to the Vietnamese instead of to the Cambodians. Discrimination was practiced against the Cambodians, which prevented them from holding higher-level positions. Those were reserved for the French.

Chapter 5 – War and Politics

The 1916 Protests

Cambodia did not play a direct role in World War I, which lasted from 1914 to 1918. However, they did play an indirect part, as France used their Southeast Asian territories to help fund the war efforts. In late 1915, 300 peasants who worked near Phnom Penh met with King Sisowath to ask for a reduction in taxes, adding that they wanted the taxes to be collected by Cambodians, not French officials. Sisowath gave them only nominal acknowledgment. More and more people joined and marched to the palace. French police estimated that thousands participated, and the French who resided there also reported violence.

The gap between the income of the Cambodians and the French officials was wide. The Chinese merchants, too, benefited from the profits of Cambodia. The protests subsided somewhat when the Cambodian king toured the provinces and calmed the people. Between 1918 and 1919, there were very poor harvests and even famine throughout the countryside. Despite that, French officials and Chinese merchants continued to make a profit. Medical services were very poor, and electricity and running water were almost unknown outside of Phnom Penh.

The Assassination of the Resident-General

Felix Louis Bardez was the resident-general of Cambodia in 1923. He was very ambitious, and he noted that tax revenues were successively falling, so he reorganized the system of tax collection and supervised it directly at times. Bardez was eager to find instances in which books were doctored and compromises had been made to the tax collection procedures.

Once his activity was noted by his superiors, he was transferred to another province where tax revenues had been less than expected. As soon as he arrived, a new tax was imposed upon the people to pay for the construction of a mountain resort for French officials. When a Cambodian official tried to collect the taxes in 1925, he was severely beaten by the villagers.

During the same year, Bardez, along with his interpreter and Cambodian militiamen, visited a village where there were delinquent taxpayers. The entourage was attacked by about thirty people, and Bardez and his interpreter were beaten to death. Their bodies were then mutilated.

Crowds began to gather, mainly those who had come to hear the resident-general speak. They staged a march, demanding a remission in their taxes, but they were suppressed when more troops arrived and dispersed the crowd.

A trial was held in Phnom Penh, but high-ranking officials tried to block evidence that the Cambodians paid very high taxes per capita. French officials interfered with the defense counsel; for instance, the defense counsel's tea was poisoned, and the court stenographer was transferred to another district. Over 200 people were questioned. In the end, the prime suspect, Neou, was shot when he resisted arrest, and Chuon, his partner, was condemned to death, but only after much time had passed. The defense took the position that the whole village was at fault, as they had been provoked by an unjust system and the extreme behavior of

Resident-General Bardez, who, among other things, refused the prisoners their request to have lunch the day he died.

After the trial, a royal ordinance was passed, declaring the entire village was guilty.

Internal Improvements

Between 1928 and 1932, a railroad was built in Cambodia, which boosted Chinese and Vietnamese immigration. The Vietnamese sought employment in the urban sector, allowing the cities to grow.

The Great Depression hit Cambodia, as well as much of the world, during the 1930s, and the price of rice plummeted. Tax collection likewise fell. At the end of the Depression, the growth of maize increased substantially.

In 1939, Siam was renamed "Thailand" and took over a segment in northwestern Cambodia a few years later. They opposed the return of the French and formed several independence movements. One such group called themselves the Khmer Issarak, which means "Free Khmer," which would play an important role in Cambodian history after World War II ended.

World War II

In 1941, a year after France fell to the Germans in World War II, the Imperial Japanese Army entered Cambodia. They set up garrisons there but still allowed the French officials to remain. At this time, France was operating under Vichy France, which was essentially controlled by the Axis Powers. In 1945, a year after France was liberated, Japan overthrew the French rule in Indochina. The Japanese encouraged the current king of Cambodia, Norodom Sihanouk, to proclaim independence. Instead of naming his kingdom after Cambodia, he instead called it "Kampuchea." Japan immediately ratified Cambodian independence, establishing a consulate in the capital. In exchange, Sihanouk got rid of the previous treaties made with France and created an alliance with Japan.

At the end of World War II, in August of 1945, Japan surrendered, and the Allied military entered Indochina. Son Ngoc Thanh, the former foreign minister, made himself the new prime minister. In October of that year, French authorities returned. They arrested Son Ngoc Thanh for collaborating with the Japanese and exiled him to France. Many of his supporters joined the Khmer Issarak, as they believed in Son Ngoc Thanh's vision of a government without colonial rule.

Early Political Parties

In Phnom Penh, Norodom Sihanouk acted as the head of state and negotiated with France for independence while keeping an eye on the independence movements, which threatened to spill over into a civil war. In 1946, France allowed political parties to be formed in Cambodia and to begin drafting a constitution. These parties were the Democratic Party, led by Prince Sisowath Yuthevong, and the Liberal Party, headed by Prince Norodom Norindeth. Prince Yuthevong favored the kind of democracy practiced in France, which was preferred by the younger members of the bureaucracy. They were supporters of the Khmer Issarak movement as well. The short-lived Liberal Party was composed mostly of elderly members and landowners who wanted to preserve the status quo and slowly introduce democratic measures.

The Democrats gained the majority of seats in the Consultative Assembly, which would help guide the drafting of the new constitution, but they were fiercely opposed by Sihanouk. Sihanouk preferred the Liberal Party himself, as it would leave him with more power. Cambodia was also threatened by extremists in Vietnam, namely Ho Chi Minh and his followers, so Sihanouk didn't want to hastily expel the French. However, Sihanouk knew he was in a delicate position, as this was a tumultuous time. He realized angering the majority party wouldn't bode well for him in the long run. He agreed to the constitution, which reduced his role to that of a constitutional monarch. However, the document didn't define his role clearly, which he would later turn to his advantage.

The First Indochina War (1946–1954)

In 1946, France engaged in a war to maintain its control over Indochina, which included Cambodia, Laos, and Vietnam. France was opposed by Vietnam, namely the Viet Minh, the umbrella organization of Ho Chi Minh; the Khmer Issarak, who had been occupying sectors in northwestern Cambodia; the Pathet Lao, a communist group in Laos; and the Lao Issara, a non-communist organization. French forces included troops from Cambodia, French-controlled Vietnam, and Laos, as well as mercenary troops from other French colonies.

While Cambodians fought in the war, most of the fighting took place in Vietnam. However, there were several events that took place that greatly impacted the country. In 1950, Son Ngoc Minh, the leader of the United Issarak Front, which was made up mostly of members from the recently formed Indochina Communist Party, declared Cambodia's independence, as his group controlled nearly one-third of the country. By 1954, it is assumed that the United Issarak Front controlled half of Cambodia.

In the meantime, King Sihanouk found the war to be the perfect opportunity to flex his power. In 1952, Sihanouk made a determined speech, saying, "All is disorder. Hierarchy no longer exists. There is no rational employment of talent." He then staged a coup of his own government to rid himself of the Cabinet, which was controlled by the Democrats. He hired Moroccan mercenaries to surround the National Assembly and dismissed the Democrats. Sihanouk suspended the constitution and made himself prime minister, promising to bring full independence to Cambodia in three years.

King Norodom Sihanouk

Leftist radical Cambodian students studying in France wrote a manifesto, calling for Sihanouk's abdication and accusing him of collaborating with the French. One of the major leaders of that group was Saloth Sar, also known as Pol Pot, who would become very influential in future Cambodian politics, to put it lightly.

In January of 1953, the National Assembly didn't pass Sihanouk's budget, and Sihanouk declared martial law, arresting some Democrat members in the process. He realized that with the tensions in the country, he needed to maintain a very firm grip on his power. He justified this move to a reporter, saying, "I am the natural ruler of the country...and my authority has never been questioned."

In February of 1953, Sihanouk traveled to France. He made contact with the elderly French president, Vincent Auriol, as Sihanouk wanted France to be a future ally after Cambodian independence, and he also wanted support against the machinations of the Communist Party of Kampuchea. However, Auriol was relatively powerless, and he also looked upon Sihanouk's appeal as alarming. Sihanouk then went to Canada and the United States to publicize Cambodia's difficulty in expelling the French.

By October of 1953, the French had granted Sihanouk authority over the armed forces, foreign affairs, and the judiciary system. On November 9th, 1953, Sihanouk delivered on his promise for full independence.

End of French Colonial Rule

In 1953, the French colonial period ended, as Cambodia had gained its independence. The First Indochina War wouldn't end until the following year, and the casualties were devastating. It is estimated that around 134,500 French soldiers and their allies had died or been declared missing. The Viet Minh casualties are harder to estimate, as there are two figures for them. According to Western historians, between 175,000 and 300,000 Vietnamese died or went missing, while Vietnamese sources say it was closer to 191,000.

The war was settled with the Geneva Conference. That conference divided Vietnam into two sectors: North Vietnam, which would be controlled by the Viet Minh, and South Vietnam, which would be controlled by the dynastic Nguyen rule under Bao Dai until a democratic government could be established. Laos was also granted full independence, as was Cambodia. Sihanouk marched to Phnom Penh in triumph, becoming widely popular with the people.

New Political Parties: 1955 Elections

This was the first election after the country's independence had been internationally recognized, and many different parties took part.

The Krom Pracheachon was founded in 1954, and it declared a socialist platform. Pol Pot was involved in its foundation, and it was essentially a front for the Communist Party of Kampuchea. It only received about 4 percent of the vote.

In 1955, Norodom Sihanouk suddenly abdicated in favor of his father, Norodom Suramarit. He then founded the Sangkum Reastr Niyum (typically translated as the "People's Socialist Community"). As one might expect, it was a pro-Sihanouk party, advocating for a more conservative style of government. They did astoundingly well, earning almost 83 percent of the votes.

The Democratic Party was still around, but it had fewer members than before. Still, it did the second best in the election, winning 12 percent of the vote.

Prior to the 1955 general election, several newspapers that were critical of Sihanouk were shut down. Pracheachon candidates were harassed, and ballot boxes that most likely contained Democratic ballots disappeared. Sihanouk later admitted that fraud took place, mainly in areas where the Pracheachon would have done very well. Sihanouk's party would remain in power until 1970, dominating the political scene in Cambodia for fifteen years.

Cambodia during the Vietnam War

During this time, the eastern sectors of Cambodia were havens for pro-Communist North Vietnamese army forces and the National Liberation Front, which was also pro-Communist. Domestic politics in Cambodia became polarized, and opposition to the Cambodian government grew. The clandestine Communist Party of Kampuchea, led mainly by Pol Pot, came out of hiding. Sihanouk called them the "Khmer Rouge," meaning "Red Khmers."

The Vietnam War, also known as the Second Indochina War, broke out in Vietnam in November of 1955, although conflicts in the country had been present long before then. Both sides wanted a unified Vietnam, but they wanted Vietnam to be united in their style of government and beliefs. The Viet Cong of North Vietnam initiated a guerrilla war in democratic South Vietnam, which was led by President Ngo Dinh Diem, whose primary ally was the United States, although other countries took part on both sides. Cambodia declared neutrality, but in time, the war would spill over, affecting other Southeast nations.

In the 1958 election, there were only two parties: Sihanouk's party, the Sangkum, and the Pracheachon. As for the latter party, all but one withdrew before the election due to police repression.

In April of 1960, Sihanouk's father died, and Sihanouk had himself declared "chief of state," while his mother, Queen Kossamak, served as a ceremonial monarch.

Toward the end of the 1960s, Cambodia's economy faltered. Much of the rice crop had been illegally sold to the North Vietnamese soldiers, so the Cambodian soldiers were ordered to confiscate it and store it in government warehouses. There was a low yield in the rice and cotton crops, which was compounded by the high interest charged on loans to farmers. That created unrest and triggered riots. In 1967, a full-scale revolt broke out in Battambang. Sihanouk was in France at that time, so his prime minister, Lon Nol, declared martial law. Supposedly, the national police were offered a bounty for each rebel or leftist head they sent to the capital. Even though this might be fiction, it does help to show how the people saw Lon Nol's methods, as they were incredibly harsh.

In 1968, Lon Nol resigned due to a car accident he had been in, although it is possible his actions played a part in his abrupt departure. Lon Nol would become the prime minister again in 1969. After Lon Nol left, Sihanouk appointed some leftists to government positions in a weak attempt to show some support of the leftist movement.

Rise of the Khmer Rouge

During the 1960s, the communist Khmer Rouge (CPK) created the Revolutionary gradually created an army, which later morphed into the Revolutionary Army of Kampuchea. However, the followers of the Khmer Rouge were small in number at this initial stage, numbering somewhere between 4,000 to 5,000 men, but they were fiercely nationalistic. They had no interest in aligning themselves with North Vietnam. When Sihanouk restored Lon Nol to power, Lon suggested that Sihanouk establish relations with the US, which he did.

The Bombing Campaigns

Since the Viet Cong were harboring troops within twenty miles of the Cambodian-Vietnamese border, the United States initiated a bombing campaign called Operation Patio and Operation Menu against Viet Cong bases in eastern Cambodia in 1969 and 1970. The US backed that up with a ground offensive, which included both US and South Vietnamese troops. In 1970, US President Richard Nixon announced the entrance of American troops in Cambodia, only doing so after it had already occurred. Those campaigns were done in support of Lon Nol's Khmer National Armed Forces (FANK). Once the Americans and South Vietnamese left, the FANK was attacked by the Viet Cong and Khmer Rouge. Because of that, the US again resumed their attacks with Operation Freedom Deal, which will be covered in more depth in the next chapter.

Sihanouk publicly denounced the bombings, but it was revealed later by Peter Rodman, a US government official, that "Prince Sihanouk complained bitterly to us about these North Vietnamese bases in his country and invited us to attack them." US President

Lyndon B. Johnson heard the same from his emissary to Cambodia in 1968.

To this day, historians argue whether or not the US actually received approval from Sihanouk. Either way, the damage had been done. In fact, one of the reasons for the rise of the Khmer Rouge was the extreme antipathy they had for the US because they had carried the Vietnam War into Cambodia. It caused a great deal of anti-Sihanouk feelings and resulted in a purge of moderates, even including moderate Communists.

Chapter 6 – The Cambodian Civil War

The Coup

During the late 1960s, Sihanouk discovered that Communist China was backing the Communist Party in Cambodia and threatened to close the Chinese embassy due to the Communist propaganda China was distributing. Zhou Enlai promised Sihanouk that all future material would be sent to Cambodia's information ministry first. It was a weak promise, but it calmed Sihanouk down enough, and he allowed the embassy to remain open.

In 1968, the Khmer Rouge launched their first assault, starting the Cambodian Civil War. This will be talked about more in the next section, but it is important to note here, as Cambodia was plagued by Khmer Rouge incursions on top of the following events.

Sihanouk built two casinos in 1969, and Cambodians, who were desperate for money, lost thousands of dollars at the gambling tables, leading to a higher rate of bankruptcies and suicides. In early 1970, Sihanouk went away on yet another trip to Europe. When he returned to his country, he would find it in utter chaos.

Sihanouk had been having medical issues toward the end of 1969, and he made Sisowath Sirik Matak his deputy prime minister. When he left that October to get treatment, Sirik Matak overstepped his boundaries, telling ambassadors to contact Lon Nol, the prime minister, instead of Sihanouk, as well as closing the casinos and privatizing the banks. When Sirik Matak went to Hanoi in North Vietnam in an effort to get them to close down their bases in Cambodia, he was horrified to find that Sihanouk had agreed to house those Communist bases inside Cambodian borders. Not only that, but Sihanouk had agreed to open the port of Sihanoukville (named after himself), which he used to ship in weapons for the Vietnam War. In exchange, Hanoi agreed to buy rice at inflated prices. The Cambodian economy was faltering at the time, so Sihanouk saw that as a benefit, but these activities were abhorrent to Sirik Matak.

In March of 1970, back in Cambodia, there were massive demonstrations in Phnom Penh against the North Vietnamese. The North Vietnamese and Viet Cong embassies in Cambodia were sacked. Lon Nol stepped in, closing the port at Sihanoukville to North Vietnam and demanding that all the Viet Cong who were present in the north of Cambodia leave by March 15th of that year. Predictably, that didn't happen. On the morning of March 16th, thousands of Cambodian youths gathered around the National Assembly, clamoring for action. That same day, the National Assembly was in session to consider corruption charges against Colonel Oum Mannorine, the Secretary of Defense and Sihanouk's brother-in-law. Sihanouk, in the meantime, had left Europe and headed to potential allies for more backing instead of heading home to quell the unrest.

According to Sihanouk, Oum Mannorine had done nothing wrong. He had heard word that Lon Nol and Sirik Matak were planning a coup and had attempted to arrest them. It is possible this was true, as Oum and all of Sihanouk's loyal security men were placed under house arrest. Siri Matak then finally persuaded Lon Nol to remove Sihanouk as prime minister. Even so, Lon Nol was very reluctant to do so, and allegedly, Sirik Matak had three armed soldiers stand by while Lon Nol signed the documents approving the coup.

On March 18ᵗʰ, the National Assembly met to argue the issue. Finally, all except one member of the Assembly voted to invoke Article 122 of the Cambodian constitution, which was the no-confidence vote. Lon Nol took over as acting prime minister. Although this was, in essence, a coup, it was done rather peacefully and according to the law rather than through assassinations and violence. It also set the stage for the future Khmer Republic.

Sihanouk's mother, Queen Kossamak, was asked to leave the palace. She did so, joining Sihanouk, who was, by that time, in Beijing—the heart of Communist China. In July, Lon Nol's government held a military trial and condemned Sihanouk of treason. They sentenced him to death in absentia.

Lon Nol, Future President of the Khmer Republic

While in China, Zhou Enlai assured Sihanouk that China still recognized him as the head of Cambodia. He promised military aid to fight against Lon Nol's newly formed Cambodian government. Sihanouk announced the formation of this resistance movement in March 1970, which he called the National United Front of Kampuchea (FUNK), and endorsed the Khmer Rouge, hoping their strong base in the country would fuel his return to the throne. Khmer soldiers approved of this, demonstrating in various parts of the country. In addition, Sihanouk made an impassioned announcement via Beijing Radio for Cambodians to rebel against the coup. His supporters violently revolted in various provinces and in Kompong Cham, a city in the Mekong Delta. Two deputy members of the National Assembly were killed. The demonstrations were crushed by the regular Cambodian army, which killed several hundred and arrested thousands.

In May, Sihanouk formed a government-in-exile based in Beijing, which he called the Royal Government of the National Union of Kampuchea (GRUNK). Numerous Communist countries sided with GRUNK, leaving Lon Nol in a rough spot. Sihanouk, who had spent the last few decades fighting the Communists, was now firmly on their side.

In October of 1970, Lon Nol formally established the Khmer Republic, with him remaining as prime minister. The US provided assistance to the new government's military forces. Lon Nol appealed to the United Nations to gain support for his new government while maintaining his neutrality in the Vietnam War. He denounced interference "by foreign forces, whatever camp they come from."

The Cambodian Civil War (January 1968–April 1975)

In April of 1970, the United States and South Vietnam, in order to support their efforts in the Vietnam War, had initiated the Cambodian campaign with the aid of the Royal Cambodian Army. They started by dismantling a number of Vietnamese logistical installations in Cambodia, but many of those had already been relocated farther inland and escaped notice.

In March of 1970, the leader of the Khmer Rouge, Nuon Chea, asked that the North Vietnamese intercede and put a stop to the Cambodian army's efforts. Because of protests in America, the US pulled back their troops but still gave some support, although it was limited. Following that, the North Vietnamese attacked the Royal Cambodian Army and overtook most of northern Cambodia. Rather than rule the territory, they turned northern Cambodia over to the local Khmer Rouge.

Operation Chenla I, August 1970–February 1971

The Khmer Republic attracted thousands of young and enthusiastic Cambodians to its ranks, eventually growing to number around 250,000 by 1975. These men, of course, were untrained. Experts have said that there was a great deal of corruption in the army, and very often, the numbers of active fighters were exaggerated. The system of food and supplies was haphazard, and it was suspected that much was sold on the black market and bypassed the troops. Hence, those who were genuinely fighting to preserve the Khmer Republic were frequently deprived of rations.

Operation Chenla I started off well, with the Khmer National Armed Forces (FANK) forces capturing their objectives without much trouble. However, in January of 1971, the People's Army of Vietnam (PAVN) and the Khmer Rouge attacked the airport in Phnom Penh and virtually destroyed the aircraft there. However, this was almost a blessing in disguise, as the planes were old, reconditioned Soviet airplanes, which the US then replaced with newer models. Regardless, this move essentially ended the operation.

Operation Chenla II, August 1971–December 1971

The objective of this operation was to clear Route 6 and reopen communications with one of Cambodia's largest cities, Kompong Thon. In late August 1971, the FANK was able to capture the PAVN-held city of Barai. Heavy fighting occurred during the bloody advance on Phnom Santuk, but it was taken by September, along with the neighboring city of Tang Krasang. By late October, FANK declared the operation a success, although they hadn't truly secured the route, which proved problematic.

Soon after, the PAVN forces received reinforcements, forcing the FANK back. During the month of December alone, PAVN forces had wiped out as many as ten infantry battalions. It was a tremendous loss for the national troops.

Operation Freedom Deal, May 1970–August 1973

After the US began gradually pulling troops out of Cambodia, US actions basically focused on removing enemy supply lines, which was the stated objective of Operation Freedom Deal. However, the US soon extended the operation so forces could engage in search-and-rescue missions to retrieve downed South Vietnamese pilots. And soon after that, the operation expanded its parameters once more.

In a last-ditch effort, especially seeing as the US had left the South Vietnamese and Cambodians to fend off the PAVN and Khmer Rouge on their own, the US restarted its aerial bombings in Cambodia. Most of the flights were in support of the FANK troops. However, US Ambassador Emory Swank later admitted that they often didn't know what villages were being bombed.

When Lon Nol announced a ceasefire after the Paris Peace Accords were signed, the US bombings stopped in hopes that unity could be achieved, but the Khmer Rouge continued the fight. The US resumed bombings later that year, forcing the Communists back. Operation Freedom Deal ended in August 1973, and overall, a large number of aerial strikes had hit villages or cities containing a large number of civilians. However, when looking at the final figures of the war's death count, it is hard to distinguish which ones were caused by the US bombing campaigns and which ones were a part of the greater Cambodian Civil War. Estimates are very wide, ranging from 30,000 to 500,000, with some scholars saying the US accounted for 50,000 to 150,000 deaths. The actual number will likely never be known for sure.

The Paris Peace Accords, January 1973

On January 27th, 1973, the Paris Peace Accords were signed by the United States, North Vietnam, South Vietnam, and the provisional government in South Vietnam, which was operated by North Vietnam. The treaty stipulated that the US and its allies would withdraw from Vietnam within sixty days, prisoners of war would be returned, all foreign troops would be withdrawn from Cambodia, a ceasefire would take place in South Vietnam along specified borders, the US would oversee financial aid to all of Indochina, and a commission would be established to monitor these agreements.

A new constitution had been written a year before in April, with Lon Nol being elected as the president of the Khmer Republic soon after. It was said that the election was deliberately rigged. Political parties cropped up, as per the new constitution, but they provided no sense of unity to the country; instead, they just promoted factionalism.

This was the exact opposite of what Cambodia needed at the time, as it was already fractured. Since the Khmer Republic was so weak, the Khmer Rouge essentially controlled most of the country. Under them, religion was suppressed, and people were executed for disobeying orders or asking questions. It seems the Khmer Rouge began acting more violently toward the populace when PAVN forces began to refocus their efforts on South Vietnam. Since there was no one to police the Khmer Rouge, the members, which were led by Pol Pot, among others, could do as they wanted. As time passed, the Khmer Rouge cut ties with the North Vietnamese and Sihanouk, who had placed his bets on their alliance so he could regain the throne.

By 1975, the Khmer Republic was in shambles. Phnom Penh, which had around 600,000 people before the war, now had to accommodate two million people, mostly refugees. And when the Khmer Rouge gained control of the rivers, by which Phnom Penh mainly received supplies, it was truly the beginning of the end for the Cambodian capital.

Operation Eagle Pull, April 12th, 1975

It was quite clear to those running the Khmer Republic that its days were numbered. The Khmer Rouge continued to close in, even hitting Pochentong, the airport in Phnom Penh to which the United States sent supplies, forcing the US to suspend air traffic. They lifted this suspension a day later, as the military realized Phnom Penh would be completely lost without their aid. Unfortunately, their aid would only continue for a short time. Soon, the Khmer Rouge overran the last positions the Khmer Republic held on the Mekong, allowing the Khmer Rouge to focus all its efforts on Phnom Penh. That same day, April 1st, 1975, Lon Nol resigned and went into exile. A military advisor said of Lon Nol's resignation, "He got us all to rise up and fight. Now he's deserting us."

The United States realized it had to evacuate its men, something they had been considering since 1973. According to that plan, there were three different options. But after hearing the predictions that there would be 3,600 evacuees, which was far more than the original 400 that had been planned, the United States realized they needed a different strategy. US Marines would secure the Phnom Penh airport while helicopters would airlift evacuees from Phnom Penh, then taking them to the airport. After the drop-off, the evacuees would be sent to Thailand.

The evacuation went smoothly, although there were fewer evacuees than had been anticipated. The top Cambodian officials were not among those evacuated, as they were upset that the Americans would no longer offer support. Sirik Matak notably remarked, "I have committed this mistake of believing in you, the Americans." The only exception was Saukham Khoy, the acting president of Cambodia.

Acting President Saukham Khoy Flees the Country

https://en.wikipedia.org/wiki/Cambodian_Civil_War#/media/
File:Saukham_Koy_arrives_on_USS_Okinawa.jpg

The Fall of Phnom Penh

After the evacuees had been airlifted from the city, a Supreme Committee was gathered to rule over what was left of the Khmer Republic. The next day, April 13th, 1975, the Khmer Rouge continued its assault on the capital. The Supreme Committee, which was headed by Lieutenant General Sak Sutsakhan, decided to send a peace offer to Sihanouk, in which they would transfer power over to him while making it clear they would not be surrendering to the Khmer Rouge.

The battle continued on April 14th. In the morning, two huge bombs, which were dropped by the Khmer Air Force, exploded near Sak's office, killing several officers and wounding around twenty others. That same day, Takhmau, the capital of the Kandal

Province, which was just seven miles away from the capital, fell to the Khmer Rouge. The southern areas of Phnom Penh erupted into a fierce battle. On April 15th, with the Khmer Rouge pressing closer with every hour, Sak Sutsakhan tried unsuccessfully to make a peace offer with the Khmer Rouge, but it was ignored. On April 17th, the members of the Cabinet and the Supreme Committee realized they were only delaying fate. They decided to evacuate to the Thai border. Sak Sutsakhan and Long Boret, who had been instrumental behind the latest peace offer, remained in the capital, leaving on one of the last helicopters. Sak made it out, but Long was not so lucky. It is not known exactly what happened, but it is believed his helicopter didn't take off in time. The Khmer Rouge executed him that same day. As for Sirik Matak, he died a few days later, presumably by a firing squad.

The Khmer Rouge victoriously entered the city. They executed the remaining senior officials and FANK officers. Soon after taking the city, they told the residents of Phnom Penh that they had to evacuate because the US was going to bomb the city, telling them they could return in three days. However, this was not true, as the US had no intentions of engaging in such a campaign. The Khmer Rouge wanted to rid the city of the refugees, as they had fled from their advance, meaning they were not loyal to the cause. Over two million people were pushed out of the city, forced to march in the hot summer heat. At checkpoints, their belongings were searched, with Khmer Rouge officers confiscating whatever they wanted. It is believed 200,000 people died on this march.

Chapter 7 – Democratic Kampuchea

"Democratic Kampuchea" was the term the Khmer Rouge gave Cambodia in January 1976. "Democratic" was a deliberate misnomer. This was a communist country. All the former traditional structures of the Cambodian governments of the past were abolished. As per the Marxist-Leninist structure, the nation was a one-party state, the Communist Party of Kampuchea, and it was headed by the Communist Party's secretary general, Pol Pot. Although it wasn't officially named Democratic Kampuchea until 1976, the new government went into existence starting in 1975 after the fall of Phnom Penh.

After the fall of the Cambodian capital, the former president, Norodom Sihanouk, was called in from China to act as the new head of state. He was paraded into Phnom Penh with great pomp and circumstance.

On January 5th, 1976, the Communist Party of Kampuchea (CPK) established a constitution. Assembly members would be elected by secret ballot. A State Praesidium (an executive council) was also created, with the Kampuchean People's Representative Assembly (KPRA) selecting members every five years. However, the members of the KPRA were never elected; instead, they were chosen by the CPK, which essentially held all the power in the country.

The transformation of the country took place in stages. During the first phase, and as mentioned above, forced migrations of people took place, as the Khmer Rouge sought to empty Phnom Penh of its native people who held different political views or of the Vietnamese who lived among them. The government would control their fates, at least for those who survived. For instance, those who had technical skills were sent back to the cities to aid in factory production. Most of the urban population would be sent to agricultural communes, working fields with little knowledge of agricultural practices. The Khmer Rouge wanted the Cambodians to produce three tons of rice per hectare, which was an incredible feat even with know-how. Of course, famine was unavoidable. And to make matters worse, the government saw acts like picking wild fruit as a crime punishable by death. Workers couldn't leave the communes and had to adhere to strict rules and backbreaking long hours. In addition, the government, wishing to stay away from Western influences, relied on traditional medicine, which only helped to aid in a greater number of deaths. During the Khmer Rouge regime, it is believed between 1.5 million to 2 million people died.

In February 1976, Sihanouk was taken around the countryside, and it is said he was "shocked" to observe the relocation of the population and the conditions under which they were living. After the tour, Sihanouk tendered his resignation, which was initially refused. However, by mid-April, they had accepted it, placing Sihanouk under house arrest at his palace in Phnom Penh. He would remain as a prisoner until 1979. It seems that the removal of Sihanouk was inevitable either way, though. Earlier that year, Zhou Enlai had died, leaving Sihanouk with no protector. A confidential document that came to light years later stated, "Sihanouk has run out of breath. He cannot go forward. Therefore we have decided to retire him."

Mao Zedong, the Communist Party Chairman in China, died in September of 1976. To keep up good relations, Pol Pot, who became the prime minister of Kampuchea the following month, planned to visit Mao's successor when he was voted in and installed.

Organization and Administration

As mentioned above, all the power belonged to the Communist Party of Kampuchea (CPK). Pol Pot served both as the general secretary of the CPK and as the prime minister, holding the former until 1981 and the latter until 1979. Nuon Chea served as the CPK's deputy secretary. There were seven other high-ranking officials, and this elite group formed what is called the "Centre," the "Organization," or "Angkar." The CPK was fond of using numbers rather than titles as designations. For example, the Angkar operated out of Office 870 in Phnom Penh.

Nuon Chea, Deputy Secretary of the CPK

*https://en.wikipedia.org/wiki/List_of_prime_ministers_of_Cambodia#/
media/File:Nuon_Chea_on_31_October_2013.jpg*

The use of numbers extended to the rest of the country as well, with regions divided by number. There were no more provinces; rather, the country was divided into seven geographic zones and two special regions. The seven zones were the Northwest, the North, the Northeast, the East, the Southwest, the West, and the Center. The special regions were the Kratie Special Region No. 505 and the Siem Reap Special Region No. 106. Each of the regions was subdivided into subregions, or *damban*.

Villages were divided into groups called *krom*, which contained between fifteen to twenty households. A *krom* was led by a leader called the *Meh Krom*.

The elites, that is, those people who became prominent in the new government, were a curious admixture of those who had studied in France and/or were students of Marxist/Leninist philosophy. That included Pol Pot, of course, but there was also Ieng Sary, the minister of foreign affairs; Khieu Thirith (or Ieng Thirith, Sary's wife and Pol Pot's sister-in-law), the minister of social affairs; Son Sen, who became the minister of defense, and Khieu Samphan, who was the chairman of the State Presidium.

The Khmer Rouge Ideology

The Khmer Rouge believed in the principles of Marxist-Leninism and the teachings of Mao Zedong. This education taught that progress and change happen through successive revolutions. Some had the benefit of higher education in France, where they were taught Marxism. The Khmer Rouge also believed in their racial superiority. They banned any foreign influences, abolished the banking system, collectivized agriculture, and closed hospitals and schools. Education was virtually nonexistent. While the Khmer Rouge wanted the people to be literate and have basic knowledge, they didn't want their education to be tainted with Cambodia's past. They wanted to be in control of the information being disseminated.

The Khmer Rouge aimed to convert Cambodia into a country of obedient peasants. Agricultural products were raised in communes, and the state and its needs were more important than the family unit. If one had sex outside marriage, they could be executed, and one could only get married with the government's permission, as they didn't want people marrying outside their rank.

The Role of Women

The Khmer Rouge boasted that work "liberated women," so they worked alongside the men and even children at times. The Khmer Rouge's position on this was derived from the work of the Marxist writer Friedrich Engels in his book, *The Origin of the Family, Private Property and the State.* Engels felt that women should perform industrial work and that the belief in the importance of the nuclear family should be abandoned in favor of the state. Engels saw the implementation of this as liberating for women. He believed her liberation would take place through participation in revolutionary activities. Furthermore, Mao Zedong stated that if such a change were to take place, the abolition of the inequalities between men and women "will follow as a natural consequence of victory in the political and economic struggles."

Some historians indicate the belief was that women would be trained to be productive members of their military forces. In the beginning, women were kept to behind-the-scenes roles, such as medical work and transportation. Over time, their roles became larger, even fighting on the frontlines themselves. Sum Sreng spoke of being taken from her family at the age of fourteen and sent to the frontlines. She described having escaped and running home to her parents, whom she dearly missed. However, she was always caught and returned to her unit. "I reached home five times. One time, I was sick—shaking, cold, hot temperature. They put me in a hammock and carried me back."

Democratic Kampuchea also promulgated a policy of breaking family bonds and traditional practices. Instead, the government wanted Cambodian peasants, in particular, to focus on the needs of the nation. The forced marriages pushed women to have sexual relations with, at times, strange men, and if they refused, their husbands and sometimes even Khmer Rouge officers would rape them. Predictably, the statistics of how many women were sexually assaulted were not kept track of by the government. According to the Women and Transitional Justice in Cambodia project, which took an anonymous survey of those who lived through the Khmer Rouge regime, it is believed that almost 97 percent of women were forced into marriage. Around 80 percent of them were raped after they got married.

Military

Democratic Kampuchea maintained a large standing army called the Revolutionary Army of Kampuchea (RAK). It had 230 battalions, which were split into 35 to 40 regiments and then subdivided into 12 to 14 brigades. The units of the military were led by three-person committees, with the ranking order going political commissar, military general, and the general's deputy. The political commissar wasn't really an army commander. Instead, they were there to make sure the unit followed the party's lines and ensure the government maintained control over the army.

The RAK operated throughout the various zones of the country, with each group assigned its own zone. As a result, a warlike atmosphere prevailed. If a member or members of any of these groups were judged to be "ideologically impure," purges took place to eliminate those undesirables, with troops crossing zones to make sure discipline was served. Their first assignment was to execute the FANK officers along with their families.

International Relations

As one might expect, Democratic Kampuchea had close relations with China and, to a point, North Korea. They maintained contact with other countries as well, although very few were allowed to have embassies in the country. The only countries allowed to operate within the Khmer Rouge's borders were the aforementioned China and North Korea, as well as Egypt, Cuba, Albania, Laos, Romania, Vietnam (until the end of 1977), and Yugoslavia.

In 1977, Pol Pot made an official visit to China, where he was welcomed by Hua Guofeng, the premier of the People's Republic of China. He called Pol Pot the "Comrade from Cambodia." Pol Pot was treated to a visit to the agricultural area of China to present him with a model of agrarian accomplishment. Pol Pot also received approval for military aid from China.

Religion

Democratic Kampuchea forbade the practice of religion, as it was, like other communist countries, an atheist state. As such, persecutions of people who practiced religions, such as Islam, Christianity, and Buddhism, took place. In fact, it has been reported that almost 25,000 Buddhist monks were executed during the Khmer Rouge regime. Despite the religious ban, some people practiced their religion in secret.

The Atrocities and Genocide

It is believed the Khmer Rouge regime was one of the most brutal in recorded history, especially considering it was only in charge for around four years. A whole book could be written on the terrors the regime perpetrated against its people, so what follows only scratches the surface.

Between 1975 and 1979, the Cambodian genocide took place. They killed revered monks, attacked refugee camps, and destroyed Buddhist shrines, along with the surrounding neighborhoods. The Khmer Rouge executed the Chams and Vietnamese, as they sought to create a master race. If one spoke a foreign language, that almost always meant a death sentence. Sometimes, people were killed for wearing glasses, as that was a sign of intelligence. People could be killed for being absent at work, for scavenging for food, or for weeping over the dead. Executioners who hadn't reached their quotas were sometimes even executed. Journalists were assassinated, and babies were murdered. Despite the fact that the Khmer Rouge had control of Phnom Penh, they continually bombed it until it consisted of silent bloodied stones that couldn't speak of the horrors they'd witnessed.

Pol Pot believed that these harsh conditions, which included forced labor, starvation, and resettlement, would keep the people in line. People were overworked, and the sick were treated as if they were just a burden of society, with many of them dying. Those who were seen as non-contributors were often told, "Keeping you is no profit; losing you is no loss."

Although Article 9 of the Kampuchean constitution addressed justice and a court system, there was none. It was replaced by interrogations, security forces, and re-education centers. One such site was Tuol Sleng, which once was a high school and is now a genocide museum. There, people were tortured and forced to give up family and friends. Between 1976 and 1979, it is believed around 20,000 people were imprisoned there. In their rooms, they were shackled to prevent escape and forbidden to talk to each other, creating a true sense of isolation with no one to trust or confide in. Waterboarding was a common form of torture, as was being suffocated with plastic bags. Although the guards were encouraged to torture the prisoners, they were not supposed to kill them outright, but, of course, this still happened.

Those who died in the re-education camps, as well as others executed by the Khmer Rouge, were buried in the Killing Fields, which were located throughout all of Cambodia. Their victims would be buried in mass graves with no ceremony. Oftentimes, executions would be done with poison, sharpened sticks, or other blunt instruments, as this saved on ammunition. Sometimes, their victims would be forced to dig their own graves.

Pol Pot also regularly conducted purges. Khmer Republic officials who had served prior to the arrival of the Khmer Rouge were "tried" and executed, as were the officers of the FANK, who had served under the Khmer Republic.

There are no hard numbers when it comes to how many died under the Khmer Rouge regime. Numbers go as low as 1 million and go as high as nearly 3.5 million. Even the Khmer Rouge acknowledged 2 million people died, although they mainly contribute these deaths to the later Vietnamese invasion. It is startingly to look at these numbers, as scholars believe Cambodia had boasted a population of around 8 million people in 1975.

Historians disagree on whether what took place should be considered genocide. Some believe the actions of the Khmer Rouge didn't specifically target ethnic groups. According to Michael Vickery, these deaths were "largely the result of the spontaneous excesses of a vengeful, undisciplined peasant army." However, recent documents have come to light, showing that the Khmer Rouge willingly engaged in systematic mass killings. Even historian David Chandler states that ethnic minorities were not targeted specifically, but that doesn't seem to be the case. For instance, it has been estimated that half of the Cham Muslim population were killed during the Cambodian genocide. They were not allowed to practice their religion and were forced to eat pork, which goes against one of the tenets of Islam. If they refused to eat it, they were killed. They couldn't practice their language, and their children were taken to be raised as Khmers. The Chams were even renamed to Islamic Khmers, further stripping them of their heritage and ethnicity.

Victims of the Ba Chuc Massacre

https://en.wikipedia.org/wiki/CambodiaVietnamese_War#/media/File: Hài_cốt.jpg

The Ba Chuc Massacre

From April 18th to April 30th, 1978, 3,157 civilians were brutally slaughtered in Ba Chuc, Vietnam. An additional 200 were either blown up or injured by land mines. It is believed only two people survived the massacre.

One of the survivors, a woman named Ha Thi Nga, said, "They shot my children one by one. My youngest, a two-year-old girl, was beaten three times but did not die, so they slammed her against a wall until she was dead." Her husband was shot and killed, and the soldiers tried to do the same to her. When the bullet didn't kill her, the soldiers bashed her in the head, leaving her to die. Miraculously, she survived.

This attack helped prompt the Vietnamese invasion of Cambodia, which took place later that year.

The KUFNS

The acronym of KUFNS, also known by the French acronym of FUNSK, stood for the Kampuchea (or Khmer) United Front for National Salvation. It was a dissident group of Cambodians who were at odds with the leadership of Pol Pot. Their influence quickly spread, both in Cambodia and in Vietnam, after its formation at the beginning of December of 1978. It seems many people were not opposed to overturning Pol Pot's brutal government of repression.

The Salvation Front was also communist, but it opposed many of the principles extolled by the Communist Party of Kampuchea. Their goal was to rebuild the Cambodian areas that had been devastated by the many battles.

The KUFNS was led by Heng Samrin, who was the chairman, and Pen Sovan, who was the vice president. They played a vital role in the outcome of the fermenting hostilities.

Cambodian-Vietnamese War, December 1978–September 1989

The third phase of Democratic Kampuchea manifested Pol Pot's deeply held suspicions of the Vietnamese. In fact, among the people who were purged were Vietnamese minorities who lived in Cambodia. He distrusted the Communist Party of Vietnam, which only increased when Vietnam signed a treaty of cooperation with Laos in 1977.

In 1977, tensions escalated between Vietnam and Kampuchea. By the end of the war, the Vietnamese were victorious over the Kampuchean troops. By early January 1978, the Vietnamese forces were only twenty-four miles away from Phnom Penh, but Vietnam withdrew its men. Despite this, Kampuchea declared it had won a major victory, even going on to claim that one Kampuchean soldier was equal to thirty Vietnamese soldiers. However, the Vietnamese, although they were poor, were well fed, while the Cambodians were half-starved. Vietnam also had more men standing by to fight (615,000 compared to Kampuchea's 70,000), as well as more tanks and aircraft. Regardless, Kampuchea pushed on, holding Vietnamese territories and overrunning outposts in Ha Tien Province.

The clashes continued throughout the year while peace talks were attempted. However, there was no placating either side. By the end of the year, China was helping bolster Kampuchea's troops. The war itself officially broke out on December 21ˢᵗ, 1978, when Vietnam sent in two divisions across the Cambodian-Vietnamese border, moving toward the town of Kratie in eastern Cambodia. The Kampuchean Revolutionary Army (KRA) wasn't able to repel the attack. Seeing the KRA's weakness, the People's Army of Vietnam (PAVN) launched a full-scale invasion, which consisted of around 150,000 soldiers, as well as heavy artillery and air support. The KRA fought back, even engaging in hand-to-hand combat when the need arose. Half of the KRA was wiped out after two weeks of vicious fighting.

Due to the heaving fighting, most of the Kampuchean leaders moved west. And it was a good move on their part, as on January 7ᵗʰ, 1979, the PAVN entered Phnom Penh, along with members of the KUFNS. They set up a pro-Vietnamese state, which they called the People's Republic of Kampuchea.

The Khmer Rouge leaders took refuge in Thailand, and the Thai government housed them at the Khao Larn camp in Trat Province. In the meantime, the new Kampuchean government established its headquarters in Phnom Penh, where they started to rebuild the social and economic life of Cambodia. Unfortunately, the personnel who composed this new government lacked the skills and education to rebuild the country, as many of those familiar with politics and the like had been killed by the purges or fled elsewhere. In addition, there were anti-Vietnamese resistance groups that rioted against these officials.

United Nations Fiasco

The exiled Kampuchean government called for an emergency meeting of the United Nations Security Council, as Norodom Sihanouk wanted to make an appeal for the deposed government. He condemned Vietnam for violating the sovereignty of Cambodia, but he deliberately overlooked the human rights abuses that had taken place due to the Khmer Rouge. Furthermore, Sihanouk insisted that the UN not recognize this Vietnamese-installed government of Cambodia and to uspend any aid to them. While seven UN countries did approve of that resolution, the Soviet Union and Czechoslovakia opposed it, so the resolution was not passed.

In February of 1979, the new Kampuchean government and Vietnam held a meeting, after which the two signed a Treaty of Peace, Friendship and Cooperation. This treaty stated that there was a relationship between Vietnam and Cambodia. After the agreement was signed, the Soviet Union, the socialist countries of Eastern Europe, and India recognized the People's Republic of Kampuchea.

International arguments ensued, as both Democratic Kampuchea and the People's Republic of Kampuchea claimed the same seat at the UN. The UN committee in charge of such objections decided to recognize Democratic Kampuchea (Khmer Rouge) as the legitimate government of Cambodia. One of the reasons for this was China's strong support of the Khmer Rouge. In January of 1980, eighty members of the UN continued to recognize Democratic Kampuchea as the legitimate government, while the rest of the UN members recognized the new government, the People's Republic of Kampuchea.

Thailand, which had been harboring the Khmer leadership temporarily and had always feared Vietnam's expansion on the Indochinese Peninsula, demanded that Vietnam withdraw all its troops from Cambodia so the Cambodians themselves could elect a government of their own choosing. What's more, the Association of Southeast Asian Nations (ASEAN) believed the new Cambodian government would threaten the region's stability. China and North Korea agreed with this consensus.

In 1979, Deng Xiaoping was the leader of China. He rose to power after the death of Mao Zedong, whom he opposed, mainly on differences related to China's economic policies. In fact, Deng managed to manipulate the unseating of Hua Guofeng as the chairman of the Communist Party of China. Deng even told the American president at the time, Jimmy Carter, that he intended not to renew the Sino-Soviet Treaty of Friendship, Alliance and Mutual Assistance, which had been signed in the 1950s. He also announced that he was going to engage in a limited attack of Vietnam, as China supported the ousted Khmer Rouge regime. Deng also warned Moscow that, if necessary, he would launch a war against the Soviet Union. To demonstrate his seriousness, Deng stationed troops along the Sino-Soviet border.

Sino-Vietnamese War, February–March 1979

In mid-February of 1979, China attacked Vietnam. China only had 200,000 troops enter Vietnam, while Vietnam had around 70,000. The Soviets assisted the Vietnamese in the war, but they only provided non-combat support.

The Chinese attacked from the west and east. In the west, troops planned to attack Cao Bang, Lang Son, and Quang Ninh Provinces. The forces in the east aimed to attack Hoang Lien Son, Ha Tuyen, and Lai Chau Provinces.

The People's Liberation Army (PLA) of China captured the heights above Lang Son. The Vietnamese, however, avoided direct combat, instead relying on guerilla tactics. On March 6th, Lang Son was taken. That same day, Deng declared that the "gate to Hanoi" was open and that the goals of the military campaign had been achieved. As China withdrew, it destroyed infrastructure and killed livestock in Vietnam, weakening Vietnam's economy in the process.

In the end, both sides claimed victory. China said it had crushed the Vietnamese resistance, while Vietnam stated it had driven off the invading troops. Both sides have varying estimates when it comes to casualties. It is believed that China suffered 26,000 deaths, while Vietnam had between 20,000 and 30,000 deaths.

Border skirmishes between the two countries continued for about ten more years, ending when Vietnam fully withdrew from Cambodia.

Chapter 8 – Humanitarian Crisis

The Refugee Camps and the "Land Bridge"

Throughout the 1980s, and even after the Cambodian-Vietnamese War ended, hundreds of thousands of Cambodians crossed into Vietnam in search of missing relatives and friends. Those who could sought refuge overseas. About 260,000 people relocated. While this was occurring, authorities didn't make any moves against the practice of Buddhism, allowing Buddhist schools to reopen. The people tried to reestablish the trade markets and businesses. Because few farmers were able to tend to their rice crops, a widespread famine broke out. The Vietnamese forces would consume what little rice there was. When some of the Cambodians managed to migrate to Thailand, the Thai people were astonished to see how emaciated and skeletal the Cambodian people were. It is believed at least 2.5 million Cambodians were at risk of starvation in 1980.

Border and refugee camps became commonplace. Sadly, politics and rivalries caused them to mimic the conflict going on around them, as the Vietnamese and the Khmer Rouge attacked some of them. A few camps became recruiting centers for the various hostile fighting forces in Cambodia. These camps were plagued by violence, rape, infighting, and depression due to the inactivity and the emotional distress the Cambodians were trying to cope with.

However, they also provided food and a small relief of safety. The government in Phnom Penh insisted that all aid be funneled through them, but distribution problems resulted, so aid agencies created the "land bridge," which bypassed the Cambodian government. By moving products on the "land bridge," camps could receive rice and other foodstuffs more efficiently. Approximately 150,000 metric tons of rice and other food arrived at the border camps as a result of this relief measure. The hungry Cambodians brought in their oxcarts, wagons, and bicycles for the food. Some aid groups objected to this "land bridge," as they felt it might encourage trade in the black market. It is also impossible to know how much food was actually distributed, as no solid records were kept by the camps that received the aid.

<u>The Nong Samet Refugee Camp</u>

Cambodian warlords initially ran this camp, which was located just inside the Thai border. The warlords were accustomed to guerrilla warfare and ruled with an iron fist. For the most part, they controlled the food distribution.

In-Sakhan became the leader of the camp, who encouraged a thriving market, which attracted not only traders but also smugglers and black marketeers. The camp's population was a staggering 200,000. UNICEF and other aid agencies had been delivering much-needed relief to the camp, but they stopped once they heard In-Sakhan was hoarding it. Many people from Nong Samet went to a neighboring camp, as they had better luck receiving food there.

In time, it became necessary for the Thai army to remove In-Sakhan, doing so in July 1980. He was eventually replaced by Thou Thon. Thou Thon was a capable leader, and under him, the Nong Samet Camp became a recruiting center for the Khmer People's

National Liberation Front, which opposed the Vietnamese-allied People's Republic of Kampuchea in Cambodia. Thou Thon organized the members of Nong Samet, and they built roads and ditches and cleaned up sites. He created an efficient method for rice distribution, and he also chipped in with some of the work as well.

Eventually, in 1983, Nong Samet was incorporated into Site Two.

Market Stalls in Nong Samet Refugee Camp

https://en.wikipedia.org/wiki/Nong_Samet_Refugee_Camp#/media/ File:Market_stalls.jpg

Site Two Refugee Camp

This camp was on the Cambodian-Thai border, and it was the largest of the refugee camps, as it accepted refugees from other camps that had been destroyed by hostile forces. It was overseen by the Royal Thai Government, the UN, and other UN-related organizations. The refugees were primarily from the Nong Samet, Bang Poo, Nong Chan, Nam Yeun, Sanro, O'Bok, Ban Sangae, and Dang Rek camps. Site Two was not used as a recruiting base; rather, it was a civilian camp for families and supporters of the Khmer People's National Liberation Armed Forces.

The Site Two programs provided medical care, public health, construction, sanitation, and skills training. The Thai did not want these camps to be permanent settlements, so they provided training to allow the people to move on and forge their own lives. These services were provided by international organizations, which included Christian Outreach, the Catholic Office for Emergency Relief and Refugees, the American Refugee Committee, and Doctors Without Borders.

As part of Thailand's rehabilitation program, they created schools and trained teachers. By early 1989, it is believed the camp had fifty schools with around 70,000 students.

Water was perhaps one of the biggest problems at Site Two, so UNBRO (United Nations Border Relief Operation) shipped water in until they could construct a reservoir. Dried beans, eggs, rice, vegetables, fish salt, oil, and wheat flour rations were given out to the residents on a weekly and monthly basis.

There were five hospitals at Site Two, but they acted more like clinics. These hospitals were not equipped with surgical tools, so if one needed surgery, they had to go to a local military hospital.

The Khmer Police temporarily provided security, but it had to be disbanded because it often violated human rights. Eventually, the Displaced Persons Protection Unit, a paramilitary group that was created solely to provide security on the border, took over. It was their function to not only maintain order but also to protect the camp from bandits.

Khao-I-Dang Holding Center

This refugee camp was on the eastern border of Thailand and administered by Thailand's Interior Ministry and the United Nations High Commissioner for Refugees. This camp came into existence after the Khmer Rouge regime fell. This facility actually had a surgical hospital, to which severely wounded or diseased patients came from other camps.

The camp had decent drainage, roads, latrines, and water tanks. It was supposed to be a temporary holding place for those who would be repatriated to other countries, including Cambodia. Approximately 4,800 arrived on November 21st, 1979, the first day it opened, and that number rose to 84,800 by the end of the year. It hit its all-time high of 160,000 in March 1980, although it could have held as many as 300,000 people.

Resettlement Issue in the Refugee Camps

Even though some of these camps sound fairly decent, especially when compared to Nong Samet's early days, one must remember that every camp was subject to violence, with both the Vietnamese and Cambodian forces shelling them. In time, Thailand declared the camps to be closed, but desperate Cambodians bribed their way in. After the hostilities ceased, the Cambodians remained in the camps, as they feared returning to their country. Instead, they preferred resettlement elsewhere. Between 1975 and 1997, around 153,000 Cambodians would make their home in the United States, with another 53,000 moving to France.

The Restoration: People's Republic of Kampuchea

The People's Republic of Kampuchea (PRK) was a communist state that was at odds with the Khmer Rouge's Democratic Kampuchea. It wanted to put the brutality of the Khmer regime in the past and move forward.

Under the People's Republic of Kampuchea, ethnic minorities were to be respected. Those minorities included the Vietnamese living in Cambodia, the Cambodians from Thailand, the "Montagnards" of the northeast (also known as Khmer Loeu, an umbrella term for various ethnic groups), and the Cham people. There was also a Chinese minority living inside Cambodia, to whom the new republic did not extend protections, as China supported Democratic Kampuchea. As a result, the Chinese endured prejudice, and their native languages, Mandarin and Teochew, were only to be spoken among themselves.

The People's Republic of Kampuchea recognized Buddhism as the state religion. Temples were gradually rebuilt, and Buddhist festivals were celebrated. An order of monks was founded in Phnom Penh, and as time went by, other monasteries were established throughout the nation.

Since the UN refused to recognize the PRK, this government was disqualified from receiving international aid for supplies, food, and its reconstruction efforts. Of course, China refused to assist, as did the Association of Southeast Asian Nations (ASEAN). However, the Eastern Bloc countries sent a small amount of assistance. The Western nations sent most of their assistance to the refugee camps in Thailand. The United States provided $5 million per year in 1982, which was later increased to $8 million in 1984, then $12 million in 1987 and 1988, before dipping back down to $5 million again.

Due to the purges carried out by the Khmer Rouge, few Cambodian intellectuals were left in either Cambodia or in Thailand. They had very little desire to return home to Cambodia and sought new homes elsewhere, mainly in the Western countries. The PRK wanted its administrators, technicians, and bureaucrats to be adequately trained, but their efforts were hampered by the people's low level of basic education and skills. To make up for that deficiency, a number of the more promising candidates were sent to Eastern Bloc countries to study.

The Propaganda Wars

The People's Republic of Kampuchea conducted an ongoing propaganda campaign to rally national support. Billboards were papered with patriotic slogans and also depicted gruesome photos of the skulls of victims from the Khmer Rouge regime. The government further boasted that it had liberated the people from the repressive regime under Pol Pot. The annual Day of Remembrance, also called the "Day of Hatred," was instituted, with one of its slogans being, "We must absolutely prevent the return of the former blackness."

For the PRK, it was important to remind the people why it existed, especially since Pol Pot's Khmer Rouge resurfaced. During 1979, members of the Khmer Rouge began making their way back into Cambodia. They were supported by Thailand and China. This resurrection of the Khmer Rouge launched military actions along the Thai-Cambodian border, waging battles against the People's Republic of Kampuchea at various outposts.

It should be noted that Prince Sihanouk was still active during all of this. He had founded his own group, the National United Front for an Independent, Neutral, Peaceful and Cooperative Cambodia (FUNCINPEC), in 1981. By 1982, it had organized a resistance pact with the remaining members of the Khmer Rouge.

Dry Season Offensive of 1984–1985

During this offensive, the Vietnamese attacked the base camps of the anti-PRK forces who were in Cambodia, driving them into Thailand. The Vietnamese wanted to ensure they didn't enter Cambodia again, implementing the K5 Plan, which attempted to seal the entrances into the country by using trenches and minefields. However, the presence of the Vietnamese tended to ignite hostilities among the native Cambodians, so this Vietnamese assistance ended up backfiring on the PRK.

Although the PRK government had a team of military advisors from the Soviet Union, Cuba, and Vietnam, the PRK had a difficult time establishing a firm hold over the country. In 1986, Vietnam announced that it would begin to withdraw its occupation forces from Cambodia. It was a gradual withdrawal, taking place over a period of several years. In April of 1989, Hanoi and Phnom Penh jointly announced Vietnamese withdrawal from Cambodian soil.

The Nascent State of Cambodia

Starting in that same year, 1989, the Soviet Union had started to collapse and therefore couldn't offer concrete military aid to Cambodia. Thus, the PRK had to consider making serious reforms to its economy and constitution.

In 1989, the National Assembly, led by Hun Sen, who became prime minister in 1984, decided to change the name of the country to the State of Cambodia. The armed forces were renamed the Cambodian People's Armed Forces. The country also began a series of economic and constitutional reforms. Free private ownership was permitted, along with a free-market approach. It was intended as a one-party state, but it allowed the palace to remain in Phnom Penh.

Sihanouk was not invited to become a king, especially seeing as he aligned himself with Democratic Kampuchea's National Government of Cambodia, which, as one might predict, had a communist flavor. This government also directly opposed the People's Republic of Kampuchea. After a series of talks, the new Cambodian government agreed to accept Norodom Sihanouk as the head of state—not as the king—in mid-1991.

UNTAC

In October of 1991, the Paris Peace Agreements were signed, bringing an official end to the Cambodian-Vietnamese War. This coincided with the culmination of the Cold War between the United States and the Soviet Union, which would end only two months later. The meeting was fostered by the UN, which established the United Nations Transitional Authority (UNTAC) in Cambodia in 1992. Its purpose was to supervise a ceasefire, repatriate the displaced Khmers living along the Thai-Cambodian border, disarm factional politically-aligned armies, and prepare the country for free elections by 1993.

UNTAC had difficulty in getting the Khmer Rouge to cooperate, as they did not want to lay down their weapons. In 1993, general elections were held in Cambodia. About 90 percent of eligible voters participated. Norodom Sihanouk's son, Ranariddh, and his FUNCINPEC received the most votes. Hun Sen's Cambodian People's Party came in second, followed by candidates from the Buddhist Liberal Democratic Party. Prince Ranariddh and Hun Sen became the first prime minister and the second prime minister, respectively. The Khmer Rouge was formally outlawed in 1994 due to its violations of the Paris Peace Agreements.

A new constitution was drafted, and the government took the form of a constitutional monarchy, with Norodom Sihanouk as the king.

1997 Coup

Tensions between Norodom Ranariddh's FUNCINPEC and Hun Sen's Cambodian People's Party escalated over the years. On July 5ᵗʰ, military police aligned with the Cambodian People's Party surrounded a FUNCINPEC garrison and tried to get them to surrender, but they refused to do so. They also surrounded the residence of a FUNCINPEC general, but that also failed.

Hun Sen, who was away in Vietnam, returned after hearing this news and repelled the FUNCINPEC's counterattacks. The fighting lasted until September of 1997. Hun Sen then seized power, and Prince Ranariddh went into exile in Paris. Many members of the FUNCINPEC either fled the country or were shot.

In his report on human rights, Thomas Hammarberg, the United Nations Special Representative on Human Rights in Cambodia, reported that what had happened was a coup d'état. Hammarberg cited that the power-sharing formula, which had allowed for two major powers to exist at the same time, was one of the factors in the dispute. Hun Sen alleged that Ranariddh and his followers had been making alliances with former Khmer Rouge forces to fully take over the country. It should be noted that Hun Sen used former Khmer Rouge soldiers in his coup.

In 1998, the leaders of the FUNCINPEC returned for the general elections. The FUNCINPEC received 32 percent of the vote, while the Cambodian People's Party received 41 percent. The newly formed Sam Rainsy Party received 13 percent of the vote. The Cambodian People's Party didn't receive enough votes to form its own government, so it offered to form a coalition government with the FUNCINPEC and Sam Rainsy Party. However, both refused. Protests broke out, but eventually, a deal was brokered between the Cambodian People's Party and the FUNCINPEC. Hun Sen would be the prime minister (there would be no second prime minister), and Norodom Ranariddh would be the president of the National Assembly.

Chapter 9 – 21ˢᵗ-Century Cambodia

In 2004, King Norodom Sihanouk, exhausted by the political crises, especially from that of Hun Sen of the Cambodian People's Party, became ill and resigned. His eldest son, Norodom Sihamoni, succeeded him.

Sihamoni spent his youth and young adulthood in Czechoslovakia. He was educated there, attending schools for the performing arts in Prague before studying filmmaking in North Korea. He later moved to France, where he taught ballet, eventually becoming the president of the Khmer Dance Association. While in France, Sihamoni was Cambodia's delegate to UNESCO.

Sihamoni remains the king in early 2021, and his prime minister is Hun Sen, who was a former Khmer Rouge leader until he defected in 1977. He is the longest-serving prime minister in the world, having taken office in 1985. In 2017, the National Assembly voted to abolish the minority leader and majority leader positions. Kem Sokha of the Cambodian National Rescue Party (CNRP) was the minority leader, having been appointed as such following a stint in prison for refusing to appear for questioning. Later that year, Hun accused Kem Sokha of collaborating with the United States to overthrow the government. A month later, the Cambodian National Rescue Party, the main opposition to the Cambodian People Party, was banned due to these charges of treason. Charles Santiago, the chairman of ASEAN Parliamentarians for Human Rights, said this move was "the final nail in the coffin for Cambodian democracy."

Communes

The communes are administrative divisions of Cambodia. They receive support from the World Bank, which funds the communes through its Sangkat Fund, which is a part of its Rural Investment and Local Governance Project. Its objective is to help reduce the poverty level of Cambodia.

The Sla commune in Takeo Province, located at the southern tip of Cambodia, has invested the funds in building canals to irrigate the lands. Besides rice paddies, some of the lands are devoted to growing cucumbers, sugar cane, and tomatoes, which they tend to grow during the dry season. Because of the canals, the farmers were able to increase their production by 20 percent.

The building of roads has also helped to increase the profitability of these communes. The Arak Trout commune of Kampong Cham Province in south-central Cambodia can transport its crops to market more efficiently than ever before. Not only that, but there is more accessibility to schools, temples, and health centers. Fifty-five percent of the villagers have even been able to afford to build houses.

Some of the people who belong to the communes have invested the funds in youth work. The Tboung Kropeu commune in Kampong Thom Province is raising awareness related to the dangers of drug use and provides youths with education on how to avoid street and rural gangs. Gangs are quite common in Cambodia, as they can be found even in small villages and towns. Drug addiction, prostitution, and gambling are also common, but communities throughout the country have been trying to take steps to temper their influence.

OIL!

In 2000, Cambodia engaged in offshore oil exploration. Massive investments poured in, mainly from US-held Chevron Texaco, which spent over $20 million on the project. In 2006, Chevron confirmed that there were 700 million barrels of oil available and around 10 million cubic feet of natural gas.

In 2004, huge deposits of oil were discovered within the territorial Cambodia waters in the Gulf of Thailand. However, production stalled out when the government and the company failed to reach a revenue-sharing agreement. Chevron decided to sell its stake to Singapore's KrisEnergy in 2014. KrisEnergy holds a 95 percent stake in the profits from the oil production, while the government holds the rest. The oil drilling began in late 2020, and it is expected to produce 7,500 barrels a day once the initial drilling is completed and the rest of the wells come online.

According to the *Khmer Times*, Prime Minister Hun Sen announced that the Ministry of Education will use some of the profits from the oil production in Cambodia for education, primarily digital instruction, as well as developing and improving school infrastructure, including laboratories and computer rooms. However, others believe the money that comes from the oil production will only add to the corruption going on in Cambodia's government.

Khmer Rouge Tribunal: Genocide and Violations of International Law

In conjunction with the United Nations, the Royal Government of Cambodia established a national court, using both local and foreign judges, to hear cases related to the Cambodian genocide and other international violations. All of the prominent people mentioned were indicted on the same day, September 15th, 2010, with varying counts of crimes against humanity, crimes of genocide, and the like.

The Defendants

Kang Kek lew was in charge of running prison camps, including the aforementioned Tuol Sleng, where they brutally interrogated prisoners. He was sentenced to life imprisonment for violations of human rights in 2010. Kang died after serving ten years.

Nuon Chea, the late Pol Pot's right-hand man (Pol Pot died in 1998), was charged with crimes against humanity, genocide, and war crimes. He was found guilty of numerous human rights violations and was sentenced to life imprisonment in 2014. In 2018, he was found guilty of genocide against the Cham people and the Vietnamese. Nuon died in 2019 while in the midst of appealing the 2018 case.

Khieu Samphan, who succeeded Pol Pot as the head of Democratic Kampuchea in 1987, was found guilty of crimes against humanity in 2014. Like Nuon Chea, he was also found guilty of the crime of genocide against the Vietnamese and Chams. Eighty-nine-year-old Khieu is currently serving a sentence of life imprisonment.

Khieu Samphan on the Stand

https://upload.wikimedia.org/wikipedia/commons/8/89/
KSAMPHAN3July2009-1.jpg

Although Ieng Sary was charged in 2010, he died before the case could be brought to a verdict. He passed away in 2013 at the age of eighty-seven.

Ieng Thirith, Ieng Sary's wife, was charged with a whopping forty crimes against humanity and twenty-seven war crimes, as well as six counts of genocide. The aforementioned men, excluding Kang Kek lew, were charged with twelve crimes against humanity, six war crimes, and two counts of genocide. Ieng Thirith reportedly aided and abetted in the planning of and in the instigation of war crimes. In 2011, Ieng was found unfit to stand trial due to Alzheimer's, and she was released from prison in 2012. She died in 2015.

These were not the only ones to be indicted in the Khmer Tribunal. There was a total of nine people, although the remaining four were indicted in 2018 onward.

Land Seizures and Protests

The Cambodian government has reportedly engaged in corruption, including the illegal sale of land to foreign investors, which resulted in the forcible eviction of many villagers from their properties.

A Cambodian land rights activist, Yorm Bopha, rose up in protest, especially in regard to the land development around Boeung Kak Lake near Phnom Penh. She claimed that Shukaku, a company owned by a senator from the Cambodian People's Party, filled much of the lake with sand after obtaining a ninety-nine-year lease to the property. According to Amnesty International, 20,000 residents were displaced by this action. As a result of Yorm's protests, the World Bank suspended aid to Cambodia in 2011 until the situation could be resolved.

In 2012, Yorm Bopha was picked up on allegedly fabricated charges of assault on two taxi drivers. She was arrested without warrants, and she was convicted of "intentional violence with aggravating circumstances" even though the people who said she "might be" the person later confirmed that she wasn't. Amnesty International indicated that Yorm and her colleague, Tim Sakmony, who was also convicted, were "persecuted purely for their work defending the rights of those in their communities who have lost their houses through forced evictions." She was cleared in 2013 of these charges, but she was arrested again for the same offenses in 2016. She was sentenced to three years in prison and ordered to pay 2,500 US dollars (10 million riels).

Urbanization and Economy

The United Nations calls Cambodia a least developed country, meaning it meets the three criteria of poverty, human resource weakness, and economic vulnerability. Global sources have said that there is a lack of strategy on the part of the government to sustain healthy economic growth, which has resulted in the growth of poverty, congestion, crime, and violence. It has been reported that Phnom Penh has many of the same kinds of problems that affect overcrowded cities, including drug addiction and even human trafficking.

Most of the urban population lives and works around Phnom Penh, with some in secondary cities like Battambang, Siem Reap, and Sihanoukville. The cities suffer from rapid urbanization, especially in Phnom Penh and Sihanoukville, and financiers have warned that this sudden rise in urban development may lead to a real estate bubble. Overpricing is common due to speculation, which has raised concerns that limited resources will be eliminated. It has been said this also occurred in the neighboring country of Vietnam and even some areas of China.

In Sihanoukville, there is a number of casinos, which gave rise to hotels, restaurants, and tourist shops. A policy of "build first, license later" has brought about this uneven urbanization, which cannot be sustained by the available resources.

Special Economic Zones

Special Economic Zones are areas specially designated by the government where trade and business regulations differ from the normal rules. In those territories, there are incentives provided for businesses, including foreign ones, which enjoy reduced taxes and customs, as well as value-added benefits. The total investment in the special economic zones has been estimated to be about US$1.65 billion. Most of the projects were, and still are, financed and run by China.

Critical Events of 2018

Prior to the July 2018 elections, in addition to the arrest of Kem Sokha, the Cambodian government curtailed media freedom, both offline and online. In 2017, authorities closed thirty-two FM radio frequencies that carried independent news programming, targeting those that featured *Radio Free Asia* and the *Voice of America*, which are both funded by the US. A day after Kem was arrested, *Cambodia Daily* was forced to close after it featured the headline "Descent into Outright Dictatorship," which focused on Kem's arrest. Although attempts have been made to block *Cambodia Daily*'s online presence, it continues to gain subscribers. In May 2018, *The Phnom Penh Post* was bought by a Malaysian businessman with ties to Hun Sen.

The 2018 Elections

As mentioned above, the National Assembly dissolved the major opposition party, the Cambodian National Rescue Party, in 2017, essentially leaving the country with a one-party system. Large numbers of those belonging to opposition parties fled the country to avoid arrest. Although this allowed them to maintain their safety, it also permitted Hun Sen and the Cambodian People's Party to secure all 125 seats in the National Assembly. Many countries, such as the US, Canada, the European Union, Japan, and Australia, have condemned the election, while China, Laos, and Thailand were among those who supported the results.

After the scrutiny by the international community, Hun Sen eased the pressure on his political opponents. The king pardoned fourteen members of the Cambodian National Rescue Party, who had been jailed for "insurrection." Tith Rorn, who was the son of a CNRP activist, died while incarcerated. Authorities claimed he died in a fall, but an examination of his body showed a broken neck and bruising.

Human Rights Violations

In February 2018, a lèse-majesté law was passed, which makes insulting the monarch a punishable offense. This also applies to posts on Facebook.

The government has frequently resorted to repressive laws "to arbitrarily restrict the activities of human rights organizations and silence them," according to the Human Rights Watch. This includes amendments to the Cambodian constitution, one of which requires the government to take action against political parties if they do not "place the country and the nation's interest first." That statement, of course, is subject to interpretation.

In July of the following year, the Human Rights Watch claimed that two activists, Kong Raya (and his family) and Soung Neak Poan, were charged with incitement to commit a felony. Kong had participated in a commemoration ceremony for the murder of a political commentator, Kem Ley, by printing T-shirts in his memory and selling them online. Kem Ley was a prominent critic of the government, who was shot in broad daylight in 2016. Police detained Kong and some of his family members, forcing them to sign a confession. Soung Neak Poan was one of the supporters who gathered at where Kem Ley had been shot, distributing posters that called for the end of such killings. Unlike Kong, Soung refused to sign a confession.

Further, the Human Rights Watch Organization called upon the UN High Commissioner for Human Rights to "outline actions to be taken with regard to its international human rights obligations under the Paris Peace Accords signed back in 1991."

A number of countries in the European Union have threatened to eliminate special trade preferences. A European Commission was deployed to Cambodia to assess the country's compliance with its human rights obligations.

It should be noted this section only scratches the surface of what is happening in Cambodia today.

UN and International Reactions

The United States of America responded to that spate of attacks on human rights by suspending US$8.3 million in assistance programs. It also imposed visa restrictions against Cambodian officials involved with such policies. Furthermore, the US Treasury Department placed sanctions against the head of Hun Sen's bodyguard unit, the Hing Bun Hieng, for leading an "entity involved in serious human rights abuses."

Sweden, Cambodia's longest participating Western donor, stopped some of its development aid, except for research and education. The European Union, as well as its member states of Australia and South Korea, in addition to other democratic countries around the world, cut election assistance.

China, a country that has no competitive elections, praised Cambodia's elections and even sent in election observers. Japan, which did not approve of the results but is in competition with China for influence over Cambodia, provided US$7.5 million in electoral support but no election observers. In terms of aid, Japan indicated it would pledge $168 million for 2018.

China, on the other hand, sent Cambodia about $5.3 billion in investment and loan agreements. China also promised another $7 billion for new projects. In 2020, it was estimated Cambodia had an external debt of over $16.6 billion.

Deforestation

While Cambodia has been credited with being one of the world's most forested countries that have not been drastically deforested, rapid deforestation is on the rise. It is such a problem in Cambodia that there are forest rangers who patrol the wooded areas. There are many impacts that came from deforestation, including the erosion of the topsoil, increased flooding, and climate change. In 2020, *The Phnom Penh Post* reported that there were almost 9,000 cases of what they call "natural resource" crimes. According to the article, people have been removing trees from protected areas in order to clear land for illegal private ownership. National authorities have placed some of the blame upon local authorities, saying that they colluded with the perpetrators.

However, they indicated some of these crimes are occurring "because traders have come to buy timber, and as people lack jobs and owe money to banks, they have resorted to illegal logging."

Water Resource Management

In December of every year, Cambodians produce Prahok fish paste, which is a staple in their diet. The freshwater Tonle Sap is a great source of fish. However, partly due to deforestation, the level of the lake has been starkly declining. According to the magazine *ASEAN Today*, "the freshwater fish catch among some of the country's licensed fishers has dropped 31% compared to last year." Cambodia's yearly fish catch is worth approximately US$600 million annually.

Under normal conditions, the Tonle Sap drains into the Mekong River in the dry season. When monsoon season comes, the Mekong River flows backward, filling the lake back up. In 2020, the water that flowed back into the lake was down a quarter from its average levels. It is believed nearly one-third of Tonle Sap's natural habitats have disappeared between 1993 and 2018. The Fisheries Action Coalition Team reported that the level had dropped too fast for the fish to reach full maturity. One of the fishermen, Sim Suom from Siem Reap, said, "Children in this community go to work in factories now because there are no fish in the lake."

There are numerous factors that play a role in this, including climate change and the erection of two new dams in Laos.

Floating Fishing Boat on Tonle Sap

Photo: Deror_avi, CC BY-SA 3.0, via Wikimedia Commons

In early 2021, Cambodia and its neighboring country to the north, Thailand, have been inflicted with a severe ecological threat from China's decision to hold back the Mekong River at the Jinghong Hydropower Station for about a month. China claimed it reduced the water flow because of "maintenance for the transmission lines of the power grid," according to the *South China Morning Post.* John Roberts of the Golden Triangle Asian Elephant

Foundation indicated that Thailand and the countries downstream from there, including Cambodia, depend upon predictable flooding to service their harvests and fishing industry. Since the year 2008, he added that "natural floods were crucial for renewal of ecosystems and provided critical habitat for fish, waterfowl and wildlife." The activist group and the Mekong River Commission reported that droughts are occurring in the lower reaches of the river. They did, however, concede that some of that was due to climate change.

Brian Eyler, the co-head of the Mekong Dam Monitor, a project partly funded by the US State Department, warned that China's withholding of this upstream water came without sufficient warning or transparency. "No one had time to prepare for the river dropping nearly one meter overnight. China needs to provide notification in a much more timely manner and as take downstream needs into deeper consideration and demonstrate a higher level of accountability in the region," Eyler said.

According to the World Bank, there have been some recent successes in sustaining a potable water supply in Phnom Penh. They have four water treatment plants there and an envious distribution system. Critics, though, have pointed out the fact that this hasn't been done in moderately-sized cities.

In some cities, like Sihanoukville, urban development is uneven. Some constructions of high-rise developments have been too rapid, which has placed a strain on the water supply. In addition, complaints erupted when the water was cut off at various phases in the erection of these projects.

Flood Protection, Drainage, and Waste Management

The opposite problem has also occurred, as Cambodia is subject to a cycle of monsoons and dry spells. Areas around Phnom Penh and Battambang, which are on the banks of Tonle Sap, are vulnerable to floods during the rainy season. On occasion, there have been more severe monsoons and typhoons. Sihanoukville is affected adversely by a rise in the sea level, and its lack of adequate drainage is exacerbated by inadequate solid waste management. Only 44 percent of the population in the urban areas are connected to a sewer system. The remaining people use septic tanks, but it is up to the individual property owners to maintain those tanks. In Phnom Penh, there is a limited landfill capacity, and the projections of the people's needs have proven to be incorrect, as it reached capacity in 2020. The Royal Government of Cambodia has admitted it faces difficulties in the area of waste management and has called for a Wastewater Management Law to resolve this problem.

Some of the solid waste management services have been subcontracted to private companies, but they indicated that solid waste is wrongfully deposited along roadways and public spaces, particularly in Siem Reap. The government doesn't compensate those companies for their losses in their clean-up efforts, and, unfortunately, some of it remains undone.

Exports

In 2020, Cambodia exported US$4 billion in agricultural products. These exports include milled and paddy rice, mangos, cashew nuts, rubber, bananas, and Pailin longan. Pailin longan are very sweet, small, beige-colored fruits. In return, Cambodia imports vehicles, machinery, and animal feed from the US.

The *Khmer Times* reports that Cambodia exported $526 million of goods to the United States in 2020, which was a 32 percent increase from the prior year. The goods are being exported according to the Generalized System of Preferences, a bilateral trade agreement between the two countries.

Conclusion

Cambodia remains a country in crisis. Over the centuries, its soil has been trampled upon by foreigners who have made Cambodia a battleground. Through the years, Cambodia has reached out to other countries, like France, Vietnam, China, and the United States, to form mutually-satisfying alliances, only to be betrayed or abandoned in time. It is a country besieged with broken promises, but it is still often criticized because the Cambodians have found political or ideological solutions in less popular and old-time philosophies. Often, Cambodia has been promised protection in exchange for their labor and goods only to incur exploitation. Even their own leaders have done that. Much of its precious past has been shrouded due to neglect by others or its own heads of state.

The Cambodians have truly been through a lot, even in recent years. The genocidal regime of the Khmer Rouge has left a tragic and indelible mark upon the people. Because it was a battlefield for many decades, climate change and the country's perennial battle with the monsoons and dry seasons pose serious humanitarian threats they are unprepared to handle. The water management system set up by their old kings is in serious disrepair, but, with foreign help, it is in the process of rehabilitation. This has allowed for increased tourism to their country and religious sites, for Cambodia truly is a beautiful country worth exploring.

However, the Cambodians themselves are bent upon survival. Cambodia has been described by analysts as a "vaguely communist free-market state with a relatively authoritarian coalition ruling over a superficial democracy." In addition, it is alleged that Cambodia is one of the most corrupt nations in Asia. It has a low-income economy, with two million people living in poverty, and it is likely this number will increase due to the COVID pandemic. Only time will tell if the Cambodians will be able to reinvigorate their economy and embrace more democratic ideals.

Part 2: The Khmer Empire

A Captivating Guide to the Merged Kingdoms of Cambodia That Became the Angkor Empire That Ruled over Most of Mainland Southeast Asia and Parts of Southern China

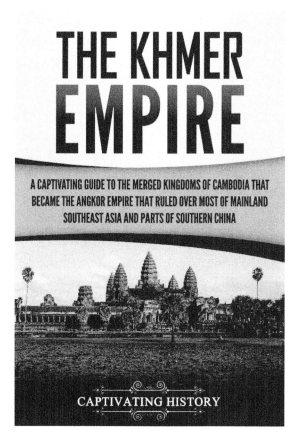

Introduction

The image of Angkor Wat, one of the greatest temples in the world, decorates the national flag of modern-day Cambodia. Cambodia is the only country in the world that has an image of ruins on its national flag, but such a thing comes naturally to this Southeast Asian country. Angkor is their heritage, their birthright, and a crucial component of their national identity. Between the 10th and 15th centuries, Angkor was the center of the Khmer Empire. It is a name of a city, a region, and the whole kingdom that once dominated the political, cultural, and economic world of Southeast Asia. The name of the capital at the time was Yasodharapura, named after its founder Yasovarman I. At its economic and social peak, the city housed over a million people, and at the time, it was one of the most densely populated cities in the world. The riches of this city and its ruler came from the understanding that manpower was more valuable than gold.

However, what we know of the Khmer civilization and Yasodharapura comes from its streets, water systems, reservoirs, and, most importantly, temples. No ordinary houses, not even the royal palace, survived the tooth of time. After all, the human habitats of all social ranks were built out of perishable materials. Only the gods and their houses were worthy enough to be built out of stone. The water systems, reservoirs, and streets were given religious meaning; therefore, they too deserved the strong and sturdy materials that can resist time. Although kings and their immediate family were depicted in stone, they were given the image of the divine. The Khmer kings are depicted in the images of Shiva, Vishnu, and later Buddha, and their ancestors were depicted as the various aspects of the divine. The crown jewel of the Empire of Angkor was its temple, Angkor Wat.

Angkor Wat, which was built in the 12th century as the monument to King Suryavarman II and also served as his tomb, breaks the tradition of Hindu Shaivism. It was almost as if the temple was built in a different order and with a different organization and orientation, as it breaks all the rules of the Khmer culture. Or at least so it seemed to the unwise eye of the Western scholars who tried to unravel its mysteries. Angkor Wat stands witness to the new religious ideology of the Khmer civilization, for it is a symbol of Vaishnavism. It seems as if Suryavarman II's reign came as a turning point for the whole Khmer Empire.

The Khmer Empire, also known as the Empire of Angkor, wasn't an empire in the modern sense of the word. It can hardly be called a kingdom in Western views. It is a designation given to the Khmer civilization that prospered between the 10th and 15th centuries to differentiate it from other periods of Cambodian history. Nevertheless, the Khmer Empire was a complex civilization, with the kings at the very top of society. The people warred with the neighboring tribes, worked their land and grew rice, and were builders responsible for one of the most elaborate complexes of temples and monuments in the world. The Khmer Empire was a nation of slaves and rulers, of Hinduism and Buddhism, of tradition and innovative engineering—truly, the Khmer people of the Empire of Angkor were a paradoxical entity.

The late 12th and early 13th centuries saw the reign of Jayavarman VI, one of the most renowned kings of the Khmer Empire. He rebuilt the walls of Yasodharapura and founded its new center, with his Bayon Temple in the middle. He battled with the neighboring kingdoms and expanded the territory of Angkor, but after his death, the kingdom started its long and continuous downfall. Many incompetent rulers, internal succession struggles, and foreign invasions took turns inflicting damage on the Khmer, and they each influenced the destiny of this great civilization. By the 15th century, Angkor was abandoned, and a new capital was founded in Phnom Penh (where it still stands). But Angkor was never really deserted. People continued to find shelter among the walls and ruins, whether it be from wars or from natural disasters. The jungle enveloped Angkor Wat as if to protect its beauty from the desolation of time and war that raged outside its walls, only to reveal it when the people were ready to respect the works of their ancestors once more.

When Cambodia became a French protectorate, the jungle was cut down, and the ruins of the Khmer Empire saw the light of day again. The patient work of Khmer and French archaeologists brought the ruins back to life, and Angkor Wat is one of the most visited monuments in the world today, counting over 2.6 million people each year. The site is still enveloped in mysticism and spirituality, which only makes it more attractive and magical. It is no wonder people rush to sit on the stone walls and observe the glorious sunset over the lotus bud-shaped rooftops of ancient temples. It is a sight to marvel and pay honor to the glorious past of the Khmer people.

Chapter 1 – The Foundations of the Khmer Empire

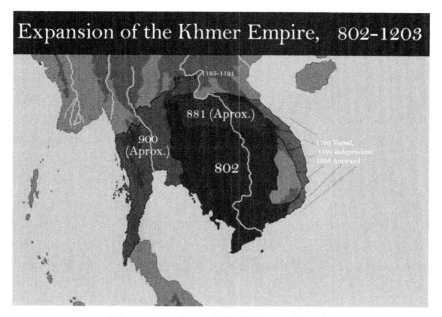

The expansion of the Khmer Empire

https://en.wikipedia.org/wiki/Khmer_Empire#/media/
File:Khmer_Empire_Expansion.png

The history of the Khmer Empire, which lasted from the 9th to the 15th century, is but a fragment of Cambodian history. The empire always referred to itself as Kambujadesa (or Kambuja), signaling it belongs to a wider historical narrative. The term Khmer Empire, or Empire of Angkor, is used today by scholars to mark the period of history in which the empire rose to power. Khmer is a name for the people of Cambodia, and even today, they represent over 90 percent of the overall population. They speak the Khmer language and are native to the South Asian mainland. Khmer people have their own origin myth that says how a Hindu Brahmin married an apsara, a celestial spirit named Mera. Out of their union, the Khmer people came to be. In the light of modern history, this myth might be a depiction of the Indianization of the native Khmer population. However, today's scholars cannot pinpoint the origins of the Khmer, and the most vocalized belief is that they are a mixture of different people of Southeast Asia, notably the Chinese and the Indus.

The history of the Khmer Empire lacks sources, and anything we know about its existence comes from the sparse stone carvings, archaeological work, and written testimonials of the Chinese diplomats and merchants. Although the 9th century is regarded as the beginning of the Khmer Empire, it is important to know the political and cultural scene of the Cambodian territories out of which the empire rose. The first document dated to the early history of Cambodia is from the 7th century, and it is written in the Khmer language. There are around two hundred such documents, some written in Khmer, others in Sanskrit. When put together, these documents give us an incomplete but realistic picture of Cambodian society of the period. The inscriptions written in Sanskrit were all written in verse, and they praised the deeds of gods and kings. The Khmer language was reserved for the documents that dealt with the common people, who were ruled by these gods and kings. This creates the image of a society divided into two parts:

those who spoke and understood only the Khmer language and those who were able to write and read Sanskrit. The Sanskrit inscriptions mainly talk about the kings who built Hindu and Buddhist monasteries and temples, the generous donations to the monasteries, and the victories in wars. Brahmins are also praised, as they were above any other social class. The Sanskrit texts are comparable to the verses written in India at the time, but the Cambodians preferred subtle words and slightly different compositions of the poetry.

Khmer inscriptions are written only in prose. They are texts that describe the founding of temples and their administration. They are the lists of people's names who are attached to the founding of certain temples and lists of a temple's inventory. They also describe the land, orchards, and rice fields in the temple's jurisdiction by listing their dimensions. From these texts, we can also learn what the duties of slaves and the amount of taxes the temples gathered were. They could be either paid in labor or in kind. These texts usually end in a curse that was supposed to threaten those who refused to abide by the temple's rules.

This division of the ancient Khmer people into two languages demonstrates the division between the rich and poor, the elite and the commoners. The elite layer of society contained the royal family and the priests. They were protected by the gods since they had direct access to them. They cherished poetry, art, intricacy, wordplay, and wealth. On the other hand, the Khmer-speaking layer of society was poor, wrote only in prose, and kept straightforward catalogs of ordinary, earthly people and possessions. These documents, both Khmer and Sanskrit, were carved in stone, usually on temple doors and columns or freestanding steles. Scholars presume these documents were also written on some kind of perishable material and were archived inside the temples, but the traces of these have not yet been found.

The duality between the languages, the social classes, and the writing material is also displayed in the use of stone. The texts were carved into stone because it was considered a divine material; thus, it was reserved only for the divine. That is why the secular buildings were never built out of stone, only the temples. Commoner's houses, dwellings of the Brahmins, and even the palace were built out of perishable materials such as wood and bamboo. The early Khmer society made a distinct difference between the earthly, perishable, and human, and the celestial, permanent, and divine. Many curses and oaths of loyalty were found inscribed on stone, presumably to make them permanent and stronger.

Aside from the social division between the elite and the commoners, there was a third group of people, but they made up only around 10 percent of society. They were the artists, clerks, concubines, artisans, high officials, and priests. During the Angkorian period, they were divided into castes or *varna*, depending on their occupation. They never served as slaves, but they were also very rarely patrons of the temples. Because of this, their names are not inscribed in stone and are forever lost. Today, we cannot know who were the artists and artisans behind the building of the great temples of Cambodia. The poor people worked the rice fields, and their only ambition was to become one of the privileged caste groups so they could get out of the muddy fields.

It is hard to translate the ancient Cambodian social terms, as their meaning is incomprehensible by Western standards. To Western society, the term "king" usually bears the connotation of medieval European kings. But in early Cambodian society, the king, or raja as they called him, has a different meaning. The raja was a ruler, but he was not what Westerners consider a king. It is a similar case for the term for slaves. In the Khmer language, this term is *knjom*, and a person designated with it had more rights than slaves of Western civilizations. But pre-Angkorian Cambodia had fourteen different categories of slaves, and it is impossible to understand them all when looked through the prism of the Western world. The slaves in old Cambodia were divided into different categories based on their origin, their social status, and the duties they performed. Perhaps the field laborers are the slave class that comes closest to the Western understanding of the term. But others, especially those attached to the temples, had different kinds of freedoms and limitations. They might have even been considered quasi-clerics. But what separated them from the free people was the fact that they could be sold and bought. They were not servants either, as they had no right to leave their service when and if they wished. If they tried to run away, they were punished.

Many of the slaves were bondsmen who worked their debt away. Some of them were even sold by their parents, and instances of hereditary servitude have been recorded. Because the slaves rarely moved and were completely attached to the territory they served in, it is possible they were never strictly attached to their owner. Generations of slaves of the same family could serve in the same territory but under different lords, but this was not always the case. Some slaves were owned by temples and by the elite members of society and were attached to their owners rather than the territory. However, it is difficult to generalize Cambodian society between the 7th and 9th centuries as the evidence is lacking. The best possible guess is that the practices varied depending on the period and the territory. Names of slaves were often written down, as they were considered possessions and had to be cataloged. Some of these names were written down respectfully, and a simple Mr. or Ms. was added to their names in Sanskrit. But the use of derogatory terms was also a norm, and many slaves were simply named "dog," "red-in-face," or "bad-smelling-one." Slaves whose names were written in Sanskrit had higher status, and they usually served as entertainers, dancers, and musicians. Their names were elaborate, poetic, and even in use today in Cambodia. They ranged from "loves justice" to various names of flowers and other botanical elements.

The Cambodian communists of the 1970s tried to represent medieval Cambodian society as being feudal, but it is clear that it wasn't. Slaves represented the majority of the population, but free peasants did exist, and they inhabited villages that were allowed to grow rice. However, the peasants had to answer the call of their rulers and join the war efforts or help in building a temple or a monastery. They were obligated to perform public works, and many of the free peasants were war prisoners or their descendants. It seems that both free peasants and slaves didn't have the aspirations for freedom and richness. They shared their masters' culture and religion, and they saw the wealth of the elite as the means of their protection. They were eager to serve, as servitude meant comfort and safety. Elevation to a better social position was possible, but it was very rare, as an individual needed a special talent and distinction. That talent also had to be recognized by the Brahmins or priests, and they rarely allowed themselves to be involved with the lower classes in the first place.

Early Cambodia's economy was based on rice. The natives were growing dry rice (flooded with rains, naturally) and root vegetables even before irrigation systems and wet rice (flooded through the irrigation system, not dependent on rain) were introduced during the Hinduization of the communities. Growing rice demands people, especially wet cultivation. People are needed to work in the mud and to maintain the irrigation system. That is why the overlordship and power in Southeast Asia, in general, meant ruling the people, not the territory. Of course, the kings and chieftains needed territory to grow rice in the first place, but the majority of Cambodia was blanketed by forests anyway, and the states had to work with what little territory they had. During the Angkorian period, the Khmer Empire extended its territory but only to the territory that could be used to grow more rice. It was only during the 12th century that the ownership of a territory became a sign of the king's prestige. But even then, it didn't last for long, as the rulers quickly recognized that it was far more important to control the people than the land.

The king was the owner of the people and the land, which was why only the king was able to grant the land for the people to use. Many Angkorian texts deal with the complicated disputes over the land and the access to it, as well as with the labor resources needed to cultivate that land. But the whole territory of Cambodia was divided into small kingdoms, or states, that were ruled by their elite. Each state had a collection of people that worked the land and could be called upon in times of war. These kingdoms traded with each other and raided each other when they were in need of more slaves. The kings of each kingdom considered themselves universal monarchs, as they were taught by Indian teachings. But they also considered themselves local chieftains according to the Cambodian tradition, as they dealt with secular tasks of the kingdom too.

The ability to lead was measured by one's success on the battlefield and his ability to attract a large base of followers. The leader also had to demonstrate his knowledge of religious rituals, and he had to protect his people in times of need. This protection wasn't only needed during times of war. The king had to be able to protect the peasants and slaves from the natural forces, the wrath of the gods, and from rival rulers. Because of this, many rulers throughout Cambodian history added the suffix *varman* to their names. It is an old Sanskrit word for defensive armor; therefore, it means protection. But rulers themselves needed protection too, and because of their high status, that protection needed to be supernatural and divine, mainly coming from the supreme god Shiva. A king's devotion to Shiva was displayed through a series of rituals that he performed to transfer the god's potency onto his kingdom and its people. These rituals included human sacrifice and were performed at the beginning of the cultivation season. Rulers used this ritual even in the 19th century. The main goal of the rituals was to transfer divine fertility onto the rice fields and on the people.

Hinduism was the main state religion of the pre-Khmer and Khmer empires. It came to the territories of Cambodia during the Funan era, which is placed between 100 BCE and 500 CE. Even when the Funan kingdom was replaced by the Khmer Empire, Hinduism remained the main religion and Vishnu and Shiva the main deities. In the 12th century, Angkor Wat was built, and to this day, it is the largest Hindu temple in the world. During the Funan kingdom and the Khmer Empire, Hindu temples were decorated with relief carvings of various scenes from the *Ramayana* (an ancient Indian epic, called *Reamker* in Khmer) and depictions of the Hindu deities.

During the Khmer Empire, Buddhism was also a popular religion. Two Khmer kings were even Mahayana Buddhists. Buddhism entered Cambodia during the Funan era, but it never became a dominant religion. After the Funan kingdom dissolved and was succeeded by the Chenla kingdom (500–700 CE), the number of Buddhists dropped significantly, but the religion managed to survive. The first kings of the Khmer Empire declared themselves as Hindu god-kings, but they were incredibly tolerant of Buddhism. They even financed their monasteries. Jayavarman VII (r. 1181–1215) wasn't the first Buddhist king, but he was the first to make it a state religion. From this point, Hinduism and Buddhism would rotate as the main state religions, but Hinduism often prevailed. During the rule of Indravarman II (1219–1243), Hinduism was again the main religion. This dualism of religion was also reflected in the temples and statues of the deities. Cambodia is full of beautiful old temples, which depict Buddha with Hindu elements or Vishnu and Shiva with the elements of Buddha. Whichever religion was dominant at the time, the holy sites were simply changed and decorated to serve the latest religious trend. Jayavarman VII, a Mahayana Buddhist himself, sent his son,

Indravarman II, to Sri Lanka for ten years, where he studied Theravada Buddhism. Eventually, when Indravarman II took the throne, Theravada Buddhism became the dominant religion, and it is believed that many social changes occurred that helped contribute to the end of the empire. Theravada Buddhism remains the dominant religion of modern Cambodia, with over 95 percent of its citizens practicing it. However, Hindu influences can still be seen in Cambodian culture.

Aside from Hinduism and Buddhism, local belief systems were also in place. These religious cults were imported mainly from China, and they represented various forms of paying respect to one's ancestors. They were always oriented toward the community, as the benefits of a whole community prevailed over the needs of the individual. These local religions often included human sacrifice among their rituals, but they mainly targeted agricultural benefits. Some of these rituals are still practiced in rural Cambodia, but they most likely have changed over time. Royals still perform the rituals in which they talk to dead ancestors to secure welfare for the whole kingdom.

The Khmer people believe in the existence of many spirits. Their ancestor spirits are probably the most widespread belief, and they are called *Nakta*. But in old Cambodia, genealogies were not kept, so these ancestors had no names. That is why *Nakta* became the ancestor spirits of the communities in certain territories. *Nakta* had the power to bring social justice to individuals and whole communities, and they also brought security, peace, and health to the community and their descendants. Although they are the spirits of the ancestors, some *Nakta* were considered wild and unpredictable. These wild spirits usually inhabited abandoned places, and the Khmer people would avoid uninhabited settlements because they believed that wild *Nakta* were too powerful and evil. Over time and due to the synchronization of the religions, local spirits in some Khmer communities received the names of Hindu gods. The temples were built on sites that were already considered sacred by the local population. In times when the influence of Hinduism and the priests declined, the local population preyed on the statues of the gods as if they were the representations of *Nakta*.

One of the Hindu cults that received a transformation among the Khmer population was the worship of lingam, a phallus-shaped stone, which represented the sexual union of Shiva and the universe. During the Angkorian era, many lingams were carved, and when Hinduism declined, the local population continued to practice its cult because of the belief that lingams were the connection between the ancestors and the earth. Wherever lingams were built, the ground around it was considered fertile and good for starting a rice field. Lingams were sometimes ceremoniously moved from one site to another, as it was believed that they brought fertility to the new location. At the same time, it was believed that the old location would lose its fertility.

Cambodia was on the main trading route between China and India, so it is not a surprise that both Hinduism and Buddhism entered the country. These religions mixed with the local cults and created a unique culture. The country is still filled with the temples in which Shiva and Vishnu took the shape of Buddha or where Buddha is adorned with Hindu symbolic ornaments.

Chapter 2 – The Founding of the Empire

Drawing of Jayavarman II praying to Shiva

The Angkorian era is roughly placed between 802 and 1431. But these years shouldn't be taken as the beginning and end of the Khmer Empire. The Khmer people lived in the area of Angkor for centuries before the state was even created. The city itself came into existence during the 9th century, and its name is a Sanskrit word meaning "city." The city was abandoned during the 15th century, but that wasn't a sudden occurrence, and there were people still living in Angkor at the time. It only lost its status as the royal city. But in the 1570s, the royal seat was returned to Angkor, although very briefly. The main temple of the city, Angkor Wat, was never really abandoned. It continued to operate at least until the 19th century, as newer statues of Buddha were found. The most recent scripture on the temple walls was dated to 1747. Even when the French archaeologists found Angkor Wat in the 19th century, the temple grounds were inhabited and maintained by several hundred slaves.

The dates that are usually taken as the beginning and the end of the Khmer Empire are nothing more than the representation of Cambodia's golden age. Between 802 and 1431, the Khmer Empire, or Kambujadesa, was the mightiest state in Southeast Asia. As such, it was a place often visited by many peoples. Pilgrims and merchants came from as far as Malaysia and Burma, as well as the kingdoms of the Thai territory to the west.

But even though the Khmer Empire dominated the whole region, we knew very little about it. We can only guess that some of its kings ruled as despots, while others didn't do anything for the kingdom. Some were completely forgotten, yet others left scores of temples, statues, inscriptions in stones, and public works. Even the administration seems to have changed over time. At some points, it was centralized and multileveled, but at other times, it seems as if the state had to oversee only several hundred followers. The history of the Angkorian period is very easy to generalize, but it is hard to understand on a deeper level. From the archaeological evidence, Sanskrit poems, and Chinese records, it is easy to see that Khmer prospered in some periods but declined in others. However, there is no evidence that explains why this happened. The Khmer scriptures left behind offer us glimpses into the cultural and material life of Cambodia at the time, but it is difficult to come to any conclusions when all a scholar has as evidence are lists of slaves, temple inventories, and royal possessions. Imagine if scholars had only decrees, deeds, and the emperors' wills as references to the whole history of the Roman Empire!

Luckily, the Khmer meticulously dated their inscriptions, so the chronological framework of Angkor is easy to deduce. Because of this, it was easy to reconstruct the chronological order in which the kings ruled the empire, even after the Cambodians themselves forgot. For this chronological reconstruction, the historians are thankful to French scholar George Coedès (1886-1968), who dedicated his life to the history of Southeast Asia. Coedès's magnum opus is the translation and dating of thousands of Cambodian pre-Angkorian and Angkorian inscriptions, which he published in eight tomes. But these inscriptions are not where we can get the information and details about the rural life of Cambodia or the life of the commoners in general. They cannot even teach us anything about the political system of Angkor as either the city or the empire. The documents rarely refer to any events, and even if they do, they are some of the more extraordinary events, such as the contracts between gods and the royal family written in Sanskrit poems or those among the people, which were written in Khmer prose.

The whole history of the Angkorian era can only be looked at through the cracks in the wall. Each crack gives us a glimpse into an event but not the context around it. We can say that the hypothetical "Temple X" was built on a certain date and was dedicated to this or that Indian god. We can see that it had this many slaves attached to it. The slaves were usually divided into lists by gender, and the children were listed by their ability to walk or if they were infants. We can also learn whether the temple grounds stretched to the east, approaching that hill, or to the west, where a certain stream or river was a border to its territories. But that is it. Temple X's context in the Angkorian period remains unknown. We will never learn how important it was or if its patrons were royals or Brahmins. Scripts like this are numerous in archaeological sites of the Khmer Empire, but they are often nothing more but stand-alone inscriptions on pieces of what used to be a temple's wall. These fragments of Khmer history became a part of the Cambodian landscape, with many monuments and steles scattered in uninhabited areas. As they were abandoned by their people and far away from their memory, temple grounds and monuments were taken over by nature.

Other than temple inscriptions, numerous temples around Cambodia still stand as witnesses to the Khmer Empire's history. They are filled with statues and bas-reliefs, as well as various artifacts. The temples tell us a story of the religious priorities of the royal family, about the popularity of myths and their meaning in the everyday life of Cambodians. From the statues, we can learn about the fashion trends of the time, as they are adorned with the popular hairstyles, pieces of jewelry, and hemlines of the period. The bas-reliefs often depict the armies, and from them, we can learn about the weapons the Angkorian soldiers used, their armor, and sometimes even their battle tactics. What the Angkorian-era documentation is missing is the larger context, a view of the overall society, politics, and culture of the period. The details about the taxes people paid, land ownership, stories of ordinary lives, and folklore remain a complete mystery.

Jayavarman II (c. 770–850; r. 802–850)

Sdok Kok Thom, an 11th-century Khmer temple in what is today southeastern Thailand, was, for a long time, a source of the chronology and history of the early Angkorian era. The inscription describes the event that took place in 802 at Phnom Kulen ("mountain of the lychees"), north of what would later become Angkor. At the mountainous city of Mahendraparvata, Prince Jayavarman Ibis took part in a ritual that transformed him from local ruler to "universal monarch." From this point, the king is known only by the name Jayavarman II. But the inscription in the Sdok Kok Thom is more concerned with describing the cult and concept of *devaraja* than with the story of Jayavarman. *Devaraja* is a Sanskrit term that can be translated as "king of the gods," and the ceremony itself was practiced to unite or somehow link the king with Shiva.

Brahmin Hiranyadama, who migrated from India, and Chief Priest Lord Sivakaivalya performed the ritual of *devaraja* to make Jayavarman a *chakravartin*, ruler of the universe. The inscription also tells us that Hiranyadama had magical powers and that he was invited by Jayavarman himself to come and help him release Kambujadesa from Javanese rule. But this *devaraja* ritual wasn't the first time Jayavarman tried to impose himself as the supreme ruler. Other scripts mention that some years earlier, in the southeast, more precisely at the cult site of Ba Phnom, the king took part in another magical ritual. This ritual was probably a part of his conquest preparations.

Jayavarman's origins are somewhere in the southeast of Cambodia, and from there, he conquered his northwestern neighbors. Jayavarman united the conquered territories, which were previously ruled under local kings. According to some historians, Vyadhapura was the first city he took before pushing his way north to Sambhupura. The king imposed himself as the ruler of the territory that is believed to be today's Banteay Prei Nokor, and from there, he launched an attack on Wat Pu, which was a royal city in modern southern Laos. From there, Jayavarman crossed the Dangrek Mountains to arrive in the region where he would start the city of Angkor. He attacked the kings of western Cambodia, but he was unsuccessful in conquering them. In fact, they defeated

Jayavarman and forced him to seek refuge at Phnom Kulen. It was during this time that the ritual of *devaraja* took place. Because of this, some historians suggest that Jayavarman performed the ritual so he could consolidate his rule over the conquered regions, as he still faced strong resistance from the west. Nevertheless, the independent kingdom of Kambujadesa was proclaimed during the ceremony, and the conquered rulers accepted Jayavarman as their superior.

According to the scripts, this whole region was previously under the control of the rulers of Java. It is widely believed that these Javanese kings actually came from the island of Java in Indonesia, but there is no evidence to confirm this claim. Alternative suggestions have been made, and some scholars believe that this particular Java could be a place in the Malaysian plains. There are no contemporary inscriptions of Jayavarman's rule, and many scholars believe that he wasn't as important a ruler as later generations made him sound. The Khmer kings that ruled after him left their written admiration of Jayavarman, as they consider him the founder of their empire. Even the Sdok Kok Thom inscription, which is considered the best source for the period of Jayavarman's rule, was carved two centuries after his rule. Some scholars even go so far as to suggest that Angkor wasn't even founded by Jayavarman.

The Sdok Kok Thom inscription also informs us that Jayavarman apparently ruled in five different regions of Cambodia at different periods of his reign. His royal cities changed from Sambor and Hariharalaya to the lost city of Amarendrapura, and that was all before 802 and the proclamation of independence. Amarendrapura is mentioned by name in the scripts, but its location remains a mystery. Some historians suggest already known places as possibilities, such as Banteay Prei Nokor or Kampong Thom, while others believe the city lays as a ruin and has yet to be discovered. It is unknown if Jayavarman built any temples, but several smaller constructions east of Tonle Sap Lake are believed to have been patronized by him.

The inscription from the 10th century suggests that Jayavarman himself came from Java, or at least that he returned from there in 770. But there is no explanation of what he was doing there. Other inscriptions mention him as being of royal descent and that he was twenty years old when he returned to Cambodia. His goal was to end the rule of the Javanese Shailendra dynasty, which possibly ruled only the southern region known as Chenla. Unfortunately, we don't know what compelled Jayavarman to pursue this course of action. It took him thirty years to achieve his goal and be crowned during the *devaraja* ritual at Phnom Kulen. We can only assume that the king used these thirty years to form various alliances through conquests, grants of land, or marriages. He possibly continued to do so after his proclamation as a "universal monarch." This would explain how he got a huge following of powerful and influential people from the region. One of the inscriptions, which are yet to be dated, claims that the borders of Jayavarman's kingdom were China, Champa, the land of cardamoms and mangoes, and the ocean. As you can see, this description of borders is not sufficient to conclude the extension of the kingdom.

Once crowned as the "universal monarch," Jayavarman slowly took over the Angkorian region. The chronology of the inscription suggests it took him around twenty years to conquer this region and assimilate it in Kambujadesa. This period is very poor with evidence, though, as it seems that only several very small and insignificant temples survived. But these years were crucial for the foundation of the Khmer Empire because, at this time, the notion of nationhood and kingship took a different shape, the one that would provide the context for the Khmer Empire through the centuries to come. We can only guess what nationhood meant for the medieval Khmer people. Maybe it was only represented in having a name for their vast kingdom, Kambujadesa, which stood in contrast to the enemy lands. The notion of kingship changed to resemble the relationship of Shiva and other gods. The universal monarch was supreme over all of his people, but he was also there to protect them. These ideas may have been imported from Java, where similar notions of a nation and kingship already existed. But due to the Funan period and the Indian influence on Cambodia, these concepts were already familiar to the local population.

It remains unclear if Jayavarman even intended to unite the Khmer people and create the Cambodians out of them or if this was a mere product of his efforts to overthrow the Shailendra dynasty. Nevertheless, somewhere along the way, the "universal king" managed to create a self-aware community that proved extremely loyal to him. The kings who followed honored Jayavarman as the founder of the nation and the kingdom. They often took a pilgrimage to Hariharalaya (present-day Roluos), where Jayavarman finally settled, to pay him respects as an ancestral founder-spirit, similar to the *Nakta* of the local people. Thus, Jayavarman II became associated with Cambodian territory as its own grand spirit that protects it.

Jayavarman's Successors

There is almost nothing known about Jayavarman's son and successor, Jayavarman III. There is some evidence that he built some of the temples dated to his rule, and one inscription even mentioned that when Jayavarman III failed to hunt an elephant, an unknown deity promised him the beast if he built a temple. Some scholars believe that he also performed the *devaraja* ritual, as the ritual itself became the symbol of legitimate rulers of Cambodia. Jayavarman's III death has been placed to the year 877. This is according to his later successor, Yasovarman I (r. 889–910), who was a very prominent ruler and builder. But even though Yasovarman started an extensive and systematic building program of temples in Hariharalaya, he mentioned his predecessor, Jayavarman III, in only one scripture. In it, he tried to link himself through family ties to none other than Jayavarman II. He claimed to be a relative of a brother to Jayavarman's III grandmother. This grandmother was the mother of Jayavarman's II wife, and it is possible she was connected to the rulers who held the region even before Jayavarman II conquered it. Yasovarman I probably wanted to legitimize his rule by linking himself to the pre-Angkorian rulers of Cambodia, but there is no evidence to explain why he needed this confirmation of his legitimacy.

At first, there was a belief that there were two more kings who ruled between Jayavarman III and Indravarman I, who took the throne directly after Jayavarman III. Their names are Rudravarman and Prthivīndravarman. They are mentioned in some Sanskrit scripts from the royal seat at Hariharalaya. However, early translators made a mistake thinking these two names were the names of kings. The inscription has been dated to the rule of Indravarman I's son, Yasovarman I, and is nothing more but a part of his meddling of the royal genealogy. A modern translation discovered that these names were mentioned to explain the family connections between the two royal families. Rudravarman was the younger brother of Jayavarman's III grandmother; however, Prthivīndravarman's connection to the royal family remains a mystery, but he might be the same individual as Prithivindreshvara, the father of King Indravarman I. The fact that both of these individuals have the "varman" suffix in their names suggests that they were indeed kings. The title "varman" could be held only by the monarch, but it seems that these two were given the title posthumously with the further purpose to legitimize the rule of the usurper Indravarman I and his son Yasovarman I.

There is evidence that suggests that Yasovarman's immediate predecessor and father, Indravarman I (r. c. 877-889), was the usurper to the Khmer throne, so this might be the reason for his extensive genealogy muddling. Indravarman I was the first Khmer ruler to start the triadic royal behavioral pattern that became a norm for the kings who followed. The first phase was to build an irrigation system in honor of his subjects and the water and soil spirits. Indravarman sponsored the construction of a large water reservoir at Hariharalaya, which was used to trap the rainwater. It covered 300 hectares (approximately 650 acres), and it was known under the name Indratataka. One of the inscriptions found in the vicinity of the reservoir mentions that as soon as Indravarman took the throne, he made a promise he would start digging the irrigation system for the rice fields in only five days.

The temple was attached to the reservoir, with the clear intention to add another layer of meaning to its construction. In the Hindu religion, reservoirs symbolized the ocean or the sacred lakes around the holy mountain. The temple attached to the reservoir was the representation of the holy Mount Meru, where the gods resided. By recreating the geographical features of the sacred mountain and the ocean or lake, the king was able to display his connection with the gods themselves, which only served to raise his prestige. This tradition is also common in northern India. The reservoirs and their temples were also places where the king and his Brahmins would perform various rituals to secure the abundant rice harvest. But the main goal of the reservoirs was a practical one. Throughout the monsoon season, they would collect water that would be released into the rice fields during the dry season. The Indratataka reservoir could hold up to 7.5 million cubic meters of water, and it was the largest reservoir at the time. Later kings built even bigger ones, making Indratataka look very small in comparison.

The second phase of the triadic royal behavioral pattern was the erection of many statues by which the ruler honored his ancestors and his parents. The statues also served as shrines, and the ancestors were given the form of gods. Indravarman built statues for his parents, grandfathers, and great-grandfathers from both his paternal and maternal sides. He also raised statues to Jayavarman II, as he considered him his ancestor, as well as to Jayavarman's wife.

All of these statues depicted the embodiment of Shiva and his consorts, and all of Indravarman's statues were built at what is today known as Preah Ko ("the sacred bull") in modern-day Roluos. This city was once the seat of early Khmer kings, and it went by the name Hariharalaya. Preah Ko was built in 879, which makes it the earliest temple built in the royal city. It consists of six towers made out of brick, which was erected in two rows. Both the front and back rows consist of three towers, but the one in the middle front row is the tallest. This tower was dedicated to Jayavarman II, and the two smaller ones next to it were dedicated to Indravarman's father and grandfather. The three towers in the back were dedicated to their respective wives. Indravarman's grandfather was named Rudreshvara, which could be the aforementioned Rudravarman who was posthumously named king by Indravarman's successor.

Preah Ko is important not only because it was the first temple built in Hariharalaya but also because it was the first built in what would become the distinct Khmer architecture of Cambodia. The temple itself was enclosed in a series of moats, and later builders would often imitate this style. The floral engraving and decoration of the temple walls suggest the transfer of the carving style from wood to stone. This is important because it suggests a major social change occurred during the rule of Indravarman, but due to the lack of any other evidence, scholars today could only guess what that change was. The fact that Indravarman's temples were more grandiose than the temples that preceded them speaks about the development of religious ideology, but yet again, the lack of evidence prevents us from understanding it completely. Later kings would overshadow Indravarman's building projects in size and beauty, but it is Preah Ko and Bakong (another temple built by Indravarman) that started the new architectural style.

One of the inscriptions at Preah Ko suggests that Indravarman became a universal monarch by fighting and defeating an unidentified enemy. At that time, Indra, an ancient Hindu deity, was tired of making so many kings, and he made Indravarman a ruler of three worlds. Indravarman's name can be translated to mean "protected by Indra," which would explain the myth behind the scripture. But which three worlds did Indravarman rule? Further examination of the inscriptions found in Rolous has led to the conclusion that he briefly led the armed forces in northeastern Thailand and the Mekong Delta. Another scripture tells a story that Indravarman ruled the lands he conquered and was the greatest king among those of China, Champa, and Java. But this doesn't necessarily mean that Indravarman ruled with higher prestige than the aforementioned kings. It was the poets' duty to decorate the king with skills, metaphors, and virtuous characteristics that would elevate him above his enemies and conceal his flaws.

The third and final phase was the building projects for the temples, which always took the shape of mountains. The king's duty wasn't only to build new temples but also to finish the ones started by his predecessors. Indravarman's temple mountain was Bakong, and it was shaped as a stepped pyramid. Unlike Preah Ko, Bakong was dedicated to Indravarman himself and was to serve his memory after his death. It is believed that these temples erected by the kings were also their burial places. There were at least thirteen kings after Jayavarman II who built these temple mountains, but not all of them survived. At first, these temples were built to resemble the holy Mount Meru, which the myths say lay to the north of the Himalayas and was the center of the universe. Since Mount Meru was the home of the gods, its replicas, in the form of temples, were homes to the king's remains. But the spirits of the kings lived together with the gods on the mythical mountain.

We don't know much about the burial practices of the Khmer Empire this early in its existence. It is presumed the king's body would have been cremated, and the ashes would have been placed in the temple mountains, which served as a sarcophagus. But it might also be that bones were placed there instead of ashes. This is a speculation based on the writings of the Chinese emissary to Angkor from the 13th century, Zhou Daguan. He described a particular practice of the Khmer people, who would throw the bodies of their dead away from the settlement to be eaten by animals. Later, they would come and pick up the bones, but for what purpose remains unknown. Zhou Daguan also attached a certain belief to this ritual. He said that people believed that if the bones were picked clean quickly, the father and mother of the deceased person were blessed. But if the animals didn't consume the body or if they only partially consumed it, this meant that the parents of the deceased were wrongdoers, and this was their punishment. Since ancestral beliefs were very strong, the punishment applied to the ancestor's spirits in case the parents of the deceased were also dead. Zhou Daguan also wrote that the kings were buried in temples, but he didn't mention if they were cremated or not.

Angkorian Khmer didn't practice burying their dead with many possessions, which is very unfortunate for archaeologists. This is also one of the reasons why so little evidence about the Angkorian civilization exists. But one Angkorian graveyard was excavated in the 1960s, located near the Srah Srang reservoir at Angkor. There, numerous cremation jars were excavated with ashes in them. Among the little items buried with the cremation jars were pieces of lead, ceramics, and bronze. This cemetery shows the signs of abandonment and renewal, as the earliest items were dated to the 11th century and the latest to the 15th century. However, there were no similar graveyards found in the vicinity of Bakong and

Hariharalaya. It might be that cremation and the burning of ashes became a practice only after the foundation of Angkor.

Bakong was the first Angkorian temple to be built out of stone. The previous temples were usually built out of bricks and perishable materials. There is also a possibility of it being the first temple of pyramidal shape, except for Ak Yom, a temple dating to the 8th century. Unfortunately, Bakong's bas-reliefs were not preserved, and the temple itself was found in very bad shape and needed reconstruction, which was performed by the French in the 1930s.

Chapter 3 – Yasovarman the Builder and His Successors

Yasovarman I (r. 889-910) was the son of Indravarman and his wife, Indradevi. He was a very important king who left behind many inscriptions and buildings. Some of the inscriptions say that he always dreamt of being greater than his father and that he started the concept of a Cambodian rule centralized around the royal city. Thus, he built his capital, which bore his name until it was abandoned in the 16th century. This capital was Yasodharapura, later known as Angkor. But Yasovarman didn't start building the city as soon as he came to the throne. He started his rule by building more than a hundred monasteries and religious hermitages. Twelve different scriptures mention this building project. Each site was equipped with a royal rest house and a set of regulations that needed to be followed. The buildings were used by the ascetics and by the king himself when he journeyed through his kingdom. The hermitages are known as *ashrams* in Sanskrit, and the term can be translated as a "step on a journey of life." These types of buildings are very common in the Hindu religion and are being built even today.

After building the *ashrams*, Yasovarman constructed an island in his father's reservoir, Indratataka. On this island, he constructed four temples dedicated to his parents. They were built of bricks and were the last temples built in Hariharalaya. Today, they are known as Lolei, which is believed to be a modernized version of the city's name. Scholars believed that the king constructed the island in the middle of the reservoir to symbolize the sacred mountain, which was, according to belief, surrounded by the oceans or lakes. The temple itself had four towers, two in each row. Each row had one tall and one short tower. The tall towers were dedicated to his grandparents, while the short ones were dedicated to his parents. The front row was built to honor the male ancestors, and the back row honors the females.

At the northeast corner of the reservoir, Yasovarman built a raised highway running toward the future site of Angkor, which was around ten miles away (sixteen kilometers). It is possible that there, at the summit of a hill, Yasovarman wanted to build his temple mountain, and because of it, the site was a natural place to build a whole city. He built his temple, Phnom Kandal ("central mountain," today named Phnom Bakheng) as his main temple, and it became one of the central pieces of the Angkor complex. He also built two more temples on the neighboring hills, Phnom Krom and Phnom Bok. The Sdok Kok Thom inscription mentioned that Yasovarman founded the royal city of Shri Yasodharapura, and here, he brought the *devaraja* from Hariharalaya, thus making it a new capital. Only then did he build the "central mountain," Phnom Bakheng.

When the first archaeologists discovered Angkor in the 19th century, Phnom Bakheng wasn't recognized for what it really was: Yasovarman's temple mountain. This discovery was made only in the 1930s when Jean Filliozat, a French scholar, made a detailed study of the temple's symbolism. He discovered that the number of levels, towers, stairways, and statues, when read together or separately, corresponds to various numbers that are considered sacred and metaphysical in Hindu culture. There are seven levels, which symbolically represent the seven heavens of Hinduism. On each level, twelve towers are present, representing the twelve years of Jupiter's journey around the sun. On top of the last level are five towers, positioned so they form a quincunx, one in the middle and four at the edges of the level. This position of the towers symbolized the five mountain peaks of Mount Meru. One hundred eight smaller towers surrounded the whole complex of the temple on the ground level. This number was not picked randomly, as it connects the sun, the moon, and the earth. The average distance of the sun and the moon from the earth is 108 times their respective diameters. The number 108 also represents the lunar cycles, as each has twenty-seven days. But only thirty-three of the towers can be seen from the temple's center, no matter what direction the observer turns to. This number represents the thirty-three gods that resided on the holy Mount Meru. Phnom Bakheng is not just Yasovarman's resting place or a temple. It is an astronomical calendar built in brick and stone. Phnom Bakheng, which was built two centuries before Angkor Wat, was the center of Yasovarman's city of Angkor.

To the east from Phnom Bakheng, a new reservoir was built by the king, and it bore his name. It was called Yasodharatataka, and it was 4 miles long (6.5 kilometers) and 2 miles wide (3 kilometers). The southern shore was reserved for the building of many monasteries, which were dedicated to Shiva, Vishnu, and Buddha. Yasovarman also ordered the construction of various temples across the kingdom, with Prasat Preah Vihear probably being the most notable one after Phnom Bakheng. It was built in the area to the north, where modern Cambodia borders Thailand. The two countries even had a dispute over the ownership of Prasat Preah Vihear, but the International Court of Justice in Hague decided that the temple belongs to Cambodia. But even though the construction of Prasat Preah Vihear started during Yasovarman's reign, the building of the temple itself is attributed to a later king, Suryavarman I. The truth is that many kings built on the site over the ages, and the temple is a mixture of architectural styles, which makes it unique among other Cambodian temples.

The scripts dating from the reign of Yasovarman give us a clue about the magnitude of his empire. The fact that he built temples all over the region he controlled also meant that he commanded a far larger pool of manpower than his predecessors. He was also a cosmopolitan ruler, aware of the grandeur of Indian civilization and tolerant of different religions. Unfortunately, the inscriptions he left behind tell us nothing about his political activity, alliances, or conflicts. There are, however, indications that Yasovarman reformed the law code of the empire so that the fine was levied according to one's ability to pay it. The taxes were efficiently collected, and they were paid in kind and labor throughout the kingdom. The Sanskrit scripts left behind glorify Yasovarman, as it was the tradition, so it is difficult to conclude how successful and efficient a ruler he was. They also fail to inform us of the king's deeds. They serve the purpose only to glorify him with epithets and metaphors. His courage is compared to that of a lion, his rule to the fangs of a beast, and his glory was similar to the roar of the king of the jungle. There is nothing substantial enough that would tell the story of Yasovarman, King of Khmer.

Jayavarman IV

Yasovarman died in 910, and his two sons succeeded him in turn. There is almost nothing known about the next two kings, Harshavarman I (910–923) and Ishanavarman II (923–928). During their reigns, their uncle, Jayavarman IV, became their political enemy. In 921, he even established his own rule in the city of Koh Ker, some sixty-two miles (one hundred kilometers) north of Angkor. This area was inhospitable, but Jayavarman IV proved his ability to lead, and he started performing kingly duties, such as building a reservoir and a temple mountain. When Ishanavarman II died in 928, Jayavarman IV took the opportunity to proclaim himself the king of the whole Khmer Empire, and he ruled from 928 until 941. His temple mountain is today known as Prasat Thom, and it housed the highest of the lingams in Cambodia except for the one in Angkor Wat. Lingams are symbols of Shiva, more accurately of his phallus inside a yoni (representation of the goddess Shakti's womb). The unification of Shiva and Shakti is a symbolic representation of creation and regeneration. The lingam at Prasat Thom used to be fifty-nine feet high (eighteen meters) and sixteen feet wide (five meters). It was probably made out of metal or at least encased in metal, but sadly, the lingam was not preserved. We only have the scripts describing it.

Koh Ker is a unique city on its own. In old Khmer inscriptions, it is known as Chok Gargyar, and this name is what makes the site unique. It is the only name in the Old Khmer language that we know, mainly because the capitals are always named in Sanskrit. The city was named after the ironwood tree (*Hopea odorata*), which is now called koki. However, the city was also named Lingapura, meaning the "city of lingams." Even when Jayavarman IV became the king, he remained in Koh Ker and made the city his capital. In his scripts, he boasted that his buildings surpassed the grandeur of his predecessors. However, Koh Ker lies largely under jungle overgrowth, so excavations have yet to be done, which will reveal the real magnitude of this city. The monuments Jayavarman IV built are among the largest found throughout Cambodia. Koh Ker alone has around forty temples, of which only eighteen are open to visitors. It is believed that Jayavarman's IV influence extended to northeastern Thailand, as several temples in the Koh Ker style have been found there.

During his reign, the focus of power shifted from the king (raja) to the kingdom (rajya). This shift of political ideology meant that the king had to do what was in the best interest of the kingdom and its people. Because of this, Jayavarman didn't go to war. His reign was the most peaceful period in the Khmer Empire's history, and he used this peace to build his empire. A cultural resurgence occurred, and society, economics, and architecture developed in a unique style. The monumentality of scale in Jayavarman's architecture, as well as the dynamism found in his sculptures, testify of his political identity. He was truly a unique Khmer king, as no one before or after him ruled in complete peace or built such grand buildings.

To build a city filled with forty temples, along with a huge number of monuments, in only twenty years, Jayavarman must have had access to money and a grand labor force. This means that he ruled over a vast empire, as he was able to bring workers from other provinces. The fact that scripts dated to his regnal years were found as far as the Mekong Delta and near Aranyaprathet testify to the extent of his kingdom. The taxes were paid in kind, as the Empire of Angkor never minted coins and didn't use any currency. But besides paying with wax, honey, animals, food, and cloth, the people were able to pay in labor and building materials. This was how Jayavarman managed to gather the workforce to build his city.

Rajendravarman II (r. 944-968) and Jayavarman V (r. 968-1001)

Jayavarman died in 941, and he was succeeded by one of his sons, Harshavarman II. However, it seems that the succession wasn't peaceful, as the new king ruled for only three years. His uncle, Rajendravarman II, fought him for the throne, managed to usurp it, and ruled the empire until 968. One of the inscriptions dated to his rule tells us how he restored the city of Yasodharapura and adorned its houses with sculptures of gold. Not much is known about Rajendravarman's rule, but he did return the *devaraja* to the old capital, making it a royal city once again. He also reverted to the old customs of building the temples in the middle of lakes, which honored the ancestors. This indicates he wanted to return to the old Angkorian kingship and not continue the ideology Jayavarman IV had started.

Rajendravarman II built many temples, especially in the north of the country. Two of them are especially prominent: the Mebon and Pre Rup, both at Angkor. The two temples are aligned with each other on the north-south axis. While the Mebon is a temple dedicated to the god Shiva, Pre Rup is the king's temple mountain where he was supposedly buried. Its modern name, Pre Rup, means "to turn the body," which comes from an old Cambodian belief that in the burial ceremony, the ashes should be carried around the temple. It is believed that Pre Rup also served as a crematorium for general use.

Although Rajendravarman warred against at least two enemies, his reign was considered to be generally peaceful. The scripts describe the king's abilities in battle and state that his sword was covered in the blood of his enemies, but there are only two mentions of conflict. The first one was against Ramanya. There is no certainty who they were, but scholars believe they could have been a Mons ethnic group of the eastern Dvaravati culture (lasted from 6th century to 11th century). It is believed that the Mons were one of the earliest builders of civilization in Thailand. The second enemy Rajendravarman fought was the Kingdom of Champa in the area between today's Cambodia and Vietnam. One scripture mentions that this last war occurred in 946 when the king took a golden statue from a Cham temple named Po Nagar.

Rajendravarman reigned during the period known for the Khmer Empire's prosperity. This prosperity is reflected in the Sanskrit scriptures left during this time. The Pre Rup stele has almost three hundred stanzas, and each one of them glorifies the king differently, from his genealogy to his wisdom and knowledge to his performances as a king. During his reign, the Khmer Empire commercially expanded to the territories of what is today northeastern Thailand. Trade was established, and with it came cultural influences. Like his predecessors, Rajendravarman was tolerant of Buddhism, and it seems he studied it himself. He even employed Buddhists in his service, for it seems that one of his ministers was one. Unfortunately, his name has been lost to time.

When Rajendravarman II died in 968, he was succeeded by his son, Jayavarman V. But at the time of his father's death, Jayavarman V was just a ten-year-old boy, and the state politics were run by his close family and high officials. We know of this because the family members left many scriptures behind them. At this point, the building of temples and statues wasn't only the duty of a king but of everyone involved in running the state. One of the most beautiful temples at Angkor, known as the Banteay Srei ("fortress of women"), was built during the reign of Jayavarman V, but the main builder was the king's relative and guru, Yajnavaraha. In fact, he was the grandson of King Harshavarman I and served as the royal doctor to Rajendravarman II. When the boy-king came to the throne, Yajnavaraha became his tutor and mentor. Yajnavaraha was a Vedic scholar, and many scripts praise his kindness and help to the poor. For his efforts to relieve the poverty across the kingdom, the guru received a present from the king, a parasol made out of peacock's feathers.

But Yajnavaraha wasn't the only one listed as the builder of Banteay Srei. His younger brother, Vishnukumura, was also listed as one of the people who commissioned the construction. Although they came from a royal family and were part of the aristocracy, they were not able to afford such extensive building projects. Because of this, the king's sister, Jahavi, was involved in the project, and she helped her cousins raise the money for the construction of the temple. Banteay Srei is a major temple in Angkor and was dedicated to Shiva. Its original name was *Tribhuvanamahesvara* ("the great lord of the threefold world"). But the temple is a complex of buildings, and while some are devoted to Shiva, others are devoted to Vishnu. The modern name of the temple, Banteay Srei, was given to the temple because of its beautiful and delicate bas-reliefs that resemble elaborate lace patterns. During the 11th century, the temple was rebuilt and expanded by later kings, and it remained in use at least until the late 14th century.

The king's sister wasn't the only female member of the royal family involved in public work. Women of the Khmer Empire were emancipated enough to take high offices, and their wisdom was often praised by foreign ambassadors. This might have been due to the influence of Buddhist teachings, which were spreading throughout the kingdom at the time. Buddha considered all people equal, and it was probably these teachings that ushered women to take on the challenge of statesmanship. Prana, another royal family member, was known for her position as the king's advisor. The Chinese scripts mention how Cambodian women of the period were emancipated and even took the positions of judges.

Jayavarman ruled in peace for the next thirty years, and no major events mark his reign. But when he died in 1001, the next few years were very destructive. The throne was succeeded by Udayadityavarman I, the maternal nephew of Jayavarman V. However, the new king reigned for only a few months before he died. Whether his death was natural or violent, we will never know. But we do know it started a civil war in the Khmer Empire, which lasted for the next nine years. His successor was Jayaviravarman, and his origins remain a mystery. Some scholars believe he was the brother of Udayadityavarman; therefore, he would have been a rightful heir to the throne. Others believe he was a usurper, maybe even a prince from Thailand's city of Tambralinga. He ruled from 1002 until 1011, and after the civil war, he simply disappears from the inscriptions.

Suryavarman I (r. 1006-1050)

After the death of King Jayavarman V, Suryavarman defeated the armies of Udayadityavarman I and proclaimed himself the king. However, Jayaviravarman claimed the throne too, and even though he took Angkor, the rest of the kingdom wasn't under his control. Suryavarman I was firmly established in the north. From there, he would launch sporadic warfare with his southern counterpart. He also formed various alliances, coalitions, and marriages throughout the kingdom, securing the support of the majority of the people. The process of his establishment as the king of the whole Khmer territory resembled that of Jayavarman II, two centuries before. It is possible that Suryavarman even had powerful allies within the priestly family of Angkor, which enabled him to eventually defeat Jayaviravarman and take his throne. Some scholars suggest that all of the previous kings that came after Jayavarman V were usurpers and that they weren't even Cambodians. According to them, Suryavarman was a local Cambodian ruler who wanted to get rid of the usurpers, although he wasn't a member of the previous royal dynasty that ruled from Angkor.

By 910, Suryavarman had defeated his enemies and established himself as king in Angkor. With his rule came a religious shift. The new king wasn't a Buddhist, but he is known for his patronage of Buddhism. Even his posthumous name, *Nirvanapada* ("the king who reached nirvana"), is an acknowledgment of his respect for this religion. Some hostile inscriptions accuse Suryavarman of destroying the religious iconography. However, if Suryavarman was of some other religion than Hinduism, the destruction of iconography would have been far more extensive. Another inscription claims that Suryavarman took away the properties and fortunes of the elite family members, as they had become rich and powerful enough to pose a threat to his rule. It seems that Suryavarman was on the constant lookout for threats, which could mean he was, indeed, a usurper.

Upon his arrival to Yasodharapura, Suryavarman demanded that all the religious and state officials swear a loyalty oath to him. More than four thousand officials gathered at the newly constructed palace to obey him. The oath they took survived in a lengthy inscription, and it ends with a threat of permanent hell for all those who break the oath. However, those who proved loyal would be rewarded with high offices, and food would be provided for their families.

Suryavarman led expansionist politics. He conquered and annexed the territories to the west. The Tonle Sap was colonized with new religious foundations, and the Theravada Buddhist kingdom of Louvo was absorbed by the Empire of Angkor. All of this led to an increase in the population, especially in the cities. The king had to expand the irrigation network to meet the demands for water. But often, Suryavarman had to defend his kingdom. There is evidence that suggests the Khmer king was forced to ask Chola Emperor Rajaraja I of Tamil Nadu (southern India) for help against the Tambralinga kingdom of the Malay Peninsula. The Tambralinga kingdom was aided by King Sangrama Vijayatungavarman of the Srivijaya kingdom (based on Sumatra). The Khmer Empire won, but this conflict led to another major one between the Chola dynasty and the Srivijaya kingdom in 1025.

Under Suryavarman's rule, the priestly and bureaucratic offices were institutionalized. But even then, they were seldom separated in practice. Government-sponsored religious foundations were used to collect revenue, but it remains obscure in what ways. However, scholars suspect that the major role was played by the powerful priestly-bureaucratic families that were close to the king. The administration of Suryavarman's kingdom focused on urbanization. The inscriptions of Suryavarman's three immediate predecessors mention the existence of twenty urban centers, which all used the suffix *pura*, which is Sanskrit for "city." This word is still in use throughout Southeast Asia and can be seen in the names of cities such as Jaipur in India or Singapore ("Lion City"). During the reign of Suryavarman, the number of cities increased to forty-seven. This means that Suryavarman led a policy of herding his subjects into tight communities. He probably uprooted them from rural areas that were hard to reach and administrate. There is a possibility that many of these settlements were cities only by name, with the intention behind it being to raise the prestige of local elite families. However, Suryavarman is responsible for the heavy urbanization of the kingdom, as other evidence suggests it too.

Some of the inscriptions that refer to King Suryavarman describe the development of local and overseas trade. Throughout Cambodian history, merchants were usually outsiders. They were native to China, Vietnam, or India, and this didn't change during the reign of Suryavarman. However, the references toward these merchants suddenly jumped in frequency. Foreign trade was largely based on exchanging wild forest goods, such as fruit and timber, for items produced by various civilizations, such as ceramics, cloth, and porcelain. However, there is evidence of trade with land, rice, domestic animals, and slaves, which were all imported from other countries. Interestingly enough, medieval Cambodians refused to implement any kind of currency, and all trade was paid in kind.

Suryavarman's urbanization of the kingdom and his ability to move and administrate the people marks a departure from the past when the economy relied on rural life. Agriculture changed too, as suddenly, one harvest per year wasn't enough to produce food for the whole kingdom. Previously, the majority of the people were commoners, and they needed less food to survive. But now, the state became a machine run by the apparatus of priests, royal family members, high officials, bureaucrats, and the army, and they all needed to be fed. The people now had to produce food all year round, a system that would remain implemented in the Khmer Empire through the reigns of the kings to come.

Suryavarman I is also remembered for the expansion work he performed on some of the already existing temples, such as Banteay Srei, Phnom Chisor, Prasat Preah Vihear, and Wat Ek Phnom. Wat Ek Phnom was used as a royal residence by the later kings. But he also built new constructions, and among the most famous was the West Baray reservoir, which was able to hold 123 million liters of water. Perhaps it was not finished during Suryavarman's reign, but West Baray remains the largest reservoir of the Khmer Empire that survived history. Suryavarman also started construction on Preah Khan Kompong Svay, around sixty-two miles (one hundred kilometers) east of Angkor. With its exterior enclosure taking up the territory of five square kilometers, it is the largest temple complex that was dated to the Angkorian era.

When Suryavarman died in 1050, he was succeeded by Udayadityavarman II (r. 1050-1066). But this new king was not Suryavarman's son. He was probably a descendant of Yasovarman I. Udayadityavarman II is remembered for finishing the construction of West Baray. However, unlike Suryavarman I, the new Khmer king didn't reign in peace. There were several rebellions, of which two were dated to 1051 and 1065. The first rebellion is described on inscriptions found at the Baphuon temple, and it mentions that the leader was a certain Aravindahrada, who was probably a vassal king of Cambodia. The king sent several military expeditions against Aravindahrada, but they all failed. Finally, when Udayadityavarman sent his loyal general named Sangrama, the rebel was defeated. The inscriptions mention Aravindahrada ran to Champa after the defeat. The second rebellion in 1065 was led by Kamvau, who was also one of the king's favorite generals. The battle between Kamvau and Sangrama is described in one of the inscriptions, and it seemed that Kamvau managed to wound Sangrama with an arrow. But Sangrama shot three arrows at his enemy, piercing his head, neck, and heart. There was also a third rebellion, led by a local chief named Slvat.

However, the date of this battle is not known with certainty. It most likely occurred in 1066, as this was the last year of Utyadityavarman's reign. Slvat had the help of his younger brother, Siddhikara, and a hero named Sagantibhuvana. Again, Sangrama managed to defeat the rebels, bind them in chains, and present them to the king.

Chapter 4 – Suryavarman II and Angkor Wat

Bas-relief depicting King Suryavarman
[https://en.wikipedia.org/wiki/Suryavarman_II#/media/File:Suryavarman_II.jpg

The last years of the 11th century in Cambodia were marked by constant turmoil and a fight for power. At some moments, three kings claimed to be the absolute ruler at the same time. Nevertheless, a new dynasty rose to power in Angkor, and it would last for more than a hundred years. Little is known about the first two kings of this new dynasty: Jayavarman VI (r. 1080–1107) and his elder brother Dharanindravarman I (1107-1113). Jayavarman VI fought Udayadityavarman II's successor, Harshavarman III (r. 1066-1080), and he managed to defeat him only because the kingdom was attacked on many sides. During the reign of Harshavarman III, the Khmers had to fight off an invasion from neighboring Champa, as well as from the Chinese Song dynasty. Finally, when faced with Jayavarman VI, who came from the Phimai area in present-day Thailand, the kingdom was already exhausted. Jayavarman VI managed to usurp the throne.

It is possible Jayavarman VI used to be a vassal prince of Cambodia, and he saw the opportunity to take the throne after the kingdom was exhausted by the constant turmoil and wars. He founded a new dynasty in Angkor, the Mahidharapura, named after his ancestral home in the Mun River Valley. The inscription found in the Phanom Rung, the temple on the edge of a volcano in Thailand, speaks about the ancient kingdom of Mahidharapura, which was probably annexed by Angkor at one point. Jayavarman VI claimed ancestry from the mythical hermit Kambu Swayambhuva, who married a nymph named Mera. His descendants were the Kambuja (Kamboja) tribe, which gave the kingdom of Kambujadesa and, therefore modern, Cambodia its name.

For the first several years of his reign, Jayavarman VI had to fight the followers of the previous king, Harshavarman III, who remained loyal to the old Angkor royal line. It is even possible that Nripatindravarman, a successor of Harshavarman III, reigned in Angkor until 1113 and that Jayavarman never really managed to usurp the Angkorian throne itself. This claim is supported by an inscription that claims Suryavarman II (r. 1113-1150) took the kingship of two kings. One was his uncle, Dharanindravarman I, who succeeded Jayavarman VI. The other one remains unnamed, but it could very well be Nripatindravarman.

Following the death of Jayavarman VI, Dharanindravarman I succeeded the throne. He married his younger brother's wife, Queen Vijayendralakshmi. There is nothing else known about the reign of this king except that he died in battle, which was fought against his great-nephew, Suryavarman II.

Suryavarman II (r. 1113–1150)

Suryavarman II was the first unifying king since Udayadityavarman II. After defeating his great-uncle, Dharanindravarman I, on the battlefield, he rose as a ruler of the unified principalities of Cambodia. He shared a name with Suryavarman I, although they were not related at all. However, the parallel between the two kings doesn't end with their names. Just like his predecessor, Suryavarman II came to power after a period of disorder, fragmentation, and internal rebellions. Once he took Yasodharapura, Suryavarman I and II both responded to disorder with vigorous administrative policies, pragmatic kingship, and expansion of territory. Suryavarman II led his forces to the east against the Champa. But these expeditions were largely unsuccessful, and the territory he gained wasn't much at all. However, it did bring new people under his control, people who would be used as a workforce behind his great building projects.

Suryavarman was crowned twice, both times by the same priest, who was named Divakarapandita. The first coronation took place in 1113, but scholars can't agree on whether Suryavarman had conquered both claimants to the throne or just Nripatindravarman. Suryavarman's second coronation ceremony took place in 1119, and some historians believe this ceremony took place because Suryavarman finally defeated Dharanindravarman I. However, the inscriptions are not clear on this matter, and it is possible that the second coronation was nothing more but the affirmation of his authority after the seizure of some Champa territory.

Suryavarman was the first king to establish diplomatic relations with China. The first embassy was sent to the Song court in 1116, where the details of trade between the two nations were discussed. The embassy stayed in China for only one year, but two more were sent in 1120 and 1128. One of the Chinese texts mentions that the Cambodian king was a great Chinese vassal. However, it is unclear if Suryavarman ever thought of himself as a servant to the Song dynasty. After all, it is no secret the Chinese emperors thought the whole world was under their vassalage.

Suryavarman warred against Vietnam and Champa because he was persuaded to do so by the Chinese. The king also used mercenaries from the western Cambodian territories in these fights and possibly even the Champa people in his attacks on Vietnam's Nghe An Province. The evidence suggests that Suryavarman was unsuccessful in his military attempts. In 1128, he sent around twenty thousand soldiers in an attack on Dai Viet, a Vietnamese kingdom. Suryavarman was easily defeated and had to flee for his life. In 1132, Suryavarman again attempted to take Dai Viet, this time by the sea. He sent seven hundred vessels, which were filled with both Khmer and Champa men, but once again, he was unsuccessful. Another expedition was sent in 1145, but King Jaya Indravarman III of Champa refused to help him, as he already made peace with the Vietnamese ruling Ly dynasty. Nevertheless, Suryavarman made one last attempt in 1150. He was defeated and had to withdraw his conquered army back to Cambodia.

Because Suryavarman II didn't want to be associated with his immediate predecessors, as they had led the kingdom into disorder, he sought to separate himself from them in religious terms. Suryavarman I did something similar when he chose to support Buddhism, but Suryavarman II did something even more drastic. He turned to Vishnu, making him the supreme deity instead of the previously worshiped Shiva. The king built some of the most impressive temples in northeastern Thailand, such as Phimai and

Phanom Rung. His devotion to Vishnu inspired him to build the largest and most beautiful of all Cambodian temples: Angkor Wat. But Angkor Wat was more than just a temple. It was a monument, a tomb, and an observatory. Today, it is one of the most visited places in the world.

Suryavarman II was the first Cambodian king who was depicted in an image. His image in Angkor Wat shows him sitting on an elaborate throne that had nagas ("snakes") instead of legs. The king himself is adorned with jewelry, such as earrings, bracelets, anklets, and armlets. In one hand, he holds a dead snake, but the symbolism behind this remains a mystery. The king's depiction is a part of a large scene that portrays court life. The scene is set amid a forest filled with attendants, princesses, Brahmins, advisors, and slaves. Suryavarman II was married, and his wife is mentioned in some of the inscriptions, but her name has been lost.

Suryavarman died in 1150 during the military campaign against Champa. He was succeeded by his cousin, Dharanindravarman II (r. 1150–1160), who was a weak ruler and who allowed the kingdom to enter yet another phase of internal feuding. Dharanindravarman married Princess Sri Jayarajacudamani. She was the daughter of King Harshavarman III. Their son, Jayavarman VII, is remembered for his devotion to Buddhism.

Angkor Wat

Angkor Wat is the temple that stands on Cambodia's national flag and is the symbol of the state, culture, and religion. It stands on 162.6 hectares of land, which makes it the world's biggest religious monument. Its construction began in the early 12th century during the reign of King Suryavarman II, who wanted a temple and a tomb for himself and his main deity, the Hindu god Vishnu. However, Angkor Wat was not completed during Suryavarman's life. The central piece of the temple, the now-lost statue of Vishnu, was erected in July 1131. Scholars believe this occurred on the king's thirty-third birthday, a number with great cosmic meaning in Hinduism as there are thirty-three Vedic deities.

Angkor Wat is unlike any other Cambodian temple, and it bears a veil of mystery. First of all, it is open to the west, while the rest of the temples are oriented toward the east. This might be because Angkor Wat was originally dedicated to Vishnu, who is often associated with the west. Cambodia's previous main deity, Shiva, is associated with the east, and all of the other temples are therefore east-oriented. And if one is to follow the bas-relief that spreads more than a mile around the outer walls of the temple, he would have to start moving counterclockwise, starting from the northwestern corner of the temple. All the other temples follow a clockwise orientation when it comes to reading the bas-reliefs, which would keep the relief on the person's right side at all times. This custom is even known in Sanskrit under the name *pradakshina* ("to the right"). But the western orientation and the counterclockwise direction is nothing new in Hinduism or the Cambodian culture. However, these practices are always associated with the dead. It is possible that because of this custom, the modern word for the west also means "to sink" or "to drown." Because of all this, some scholars believe that the primal function of Angkor Wat was to be a tomb. George Coedès, a French scholar, was the first one to suggest that Angkor Wat's orientation to the west might be connected to Vishnu, not death. But he didn't deny it could also be a tomb, as it does contain several receptacles that perhaps functioned as sarcophagi.

The original name of Angkor Wat is unknown as the foundation stele was never found. It is also odd that none of the contemporary inscriptions of Cambodia refer to this temple. Its modern name, Angkor Wat, means "temple city" or the "city of temples." Some scholars believe the old name may have been *Varah Vishnu-lok* or VARAHA VISHNU-LOK, as the temple was dedicated to Vishnu and King Suryavarman II. The king's posthumous name was

Paramavishnuloka, which means "the king who has gone to the supreme world of Vishnu." Since the temple also served as his tomb, the suggested name *Varah Vishnu-lok* is probable. *Varah*, or *Varaha*, is the wild boar avatar of Vishnu, while *Vishnu-lok* means "world of Vishnu."

Angkor Wat wasn't investigated in detail by scholars until the 1980s. This was due to World War II, the Cambodian Civil War, and the Khmer Rouge; the latter cut off the temple from the rest of the world. But the people who were allowed access brought back images and written descriptions, allowing scientists and scholars insight into the mysteries that were being kept secret in Cambodia. Eleanor Mannikka started her study of the temple's dimensions in the mid-1970s based on existing photographs of Angkor Wat. She was convinced that the learned Khmer designers of the temple had encoded it. She was the first to determine that the Cambodian measurement used at Angkor, *hat*, was equivalent to 1.3 feet (0.4 meters). She then asked herself how many *hat* were in the important dimensions of the temple, such as the distance between the western entrance and the central tower. Since the western entrance was the only one that had a causeway, its importance as a landmark was obvious. Eleanor Mannikka concluded that this distance was 1,728 *hat*. Other measurements of the important landmarks on the same axis came up with the results of 1,296 *hat*, 867 *hat*, and 439 *hat*. Eleanor Mannikka concluded that these numbers correspond to the four ages of the world, or *yuga* in Sanskrit. The first in the *yuga* cycle is *Satya Yuga* (the golden age), in which the people are ruled by the gods. It lasts for 1,728,000 years. The second one is *Treta Yuga*, a period in which Vishnu's three avatars would be seen. It lasts for 1,296,000 years. The third *yuga* is *Dvapara Yuga*, or the age of compassion and truthfulness. It lasts for 864,000 years. The fourth and last period is *Kali Yuga*, in which strife and quarrel rule. This is why this period bears the name of the demon Kali. It lasts for 432,000 years. According to

Hinduism, we are living in *Kali Yuga* at the moment. Once it ends, the world as we know it will be destroyed and rebuilt into a new golden age, and the cycle will repeat.

Eleanor Mannikka claims that the fact that the four ages closely correlate with the particular distances along the east-west axis of the temple is proof enough that Angkor Wat is coded and can be read in terms of time and space. The distance one must traverse from the main entrance to the central statue of Vishnu coincides with the *yuga* cycle and the stages one must metaphorically go through in life. Since west is seen as the direction in which the dead walk, going the opposite direction, along the west-east axis, means moving back in time. Thus, one would be approaching the golden age, at least according to Hinduism.

Mannikka worked closely with astronomers, and together, they came to interesting conclusions about the astronomical correlations of the frequently recurring distances of the Angkor Wat landmarks. The most interesting one is that if an observer stands at the western entrance on the morning of the summer solstice, he will see that the sun rises precisely above the central tower of the temple. This is important for Suryavarman II, whose name means "protected by the sun." Another interesting conclusion modern astronomers have come to is that on any other day, the sunrise aligned with the axis between the western gate and a small hill to the northeast named Phnom Bok.

Modern scholars compare the magnificence and architecture of Angkor Wat to the temples of ancient Greece or Rome. The main building material in the 12ᵗʰ century was sandstone, and the whole temple was built with sandstone blocks. The binding for the blocks still intrigues scholars as it's unknown what they used. Some think slaked lime was used, while others propose natural resins. The temple itself is typical for Khmer architecture, and it consists of lotus bud-shaped towers, the ogival half galleries, and broad passageways. The main decorative elements of the temple are bas-reliefs that depict narrative scenes, garlands, and devatas (spirits or lesser deities). Unfortunately, many of these elements were destroyed during the civil wars in Cambodia or by looters. The thieves even took some of the reconstructed figures in the hopes they could sell them as originals.

The statue of Vishnu, which is believed to have once occupied the center of the temple, was found under the southern tower. It was probably moved outside by Buddhists, who still occupy the temple. Angkor Wat is surrounded by an outer wall that is over 14.5 feet (4.5 meters) high and encloses over 203 acres (820,000 square meters), as well as a moat that is around 623 feet (190 meters) wide. The access to the temple is made out of an earthen bank and a gateway, but there are other side entrances that are big enough for elephants to pass through. Because of this, they are called "elephant gates." The temple was part of a city that also had a royal palace. However, since only the temples were built from stone, none of the other buildings were preserved. The outlines of some streets can still be seen, but nothing else except the temple itself remains.

Angkor Wat stands on a platform, raised above what was once a city. It has three galleries rising to the central tower. Each level is higher than the previous one, and they were maybe even dedicated to the king, the moon, and Vishnu. However, the temple is best known for its bas-reliefs. The inner wall of the outer gallery depicts the scenes from the *Ramayana* and *Mahabharata*. The western gallery displays the scenes of the Battle of Lanka (from the *Ramayana*) and the Battle of Kurukshetra (from the *Mahabharata*). The southern gallery wall displays a historical scene, the procession of Suryavarman II, followed by the thirty-two hells and thirty-seven heavens of Hindu religion. The eastern gallery displays one of the most famous scenes, the Samudra Manthan (the churning of the sea of milk). In this scene, Vishnu instructs ninety-two asuras (demigods) and eighty-eight devas (divinities) to churn the sea by using the body of Vasuki, a serpent king.

Angkor Wat underwent restoration works in 1986 and 1992. It is still undergoing various reconstruction projects, but it is mainly a tourist attraction. The Cambodian government protects the site, and it became a part of the UNESCO World Heritage List in 1992. In 2018, the temple saw 7,300 tourists every day of the year, making it a total of 2.6 million people. Luckily, there are no examples of tourists damaging the site, except for a few cases of graffiti. To protect the temple itself, the Cambodian government invested in ropes and wooden steps, and approximately 28 percent of the ticket revenue is reserved for temple maintenance. At least five tourists per year are caught taking nude photographs on the site of Angkor Wat, and for that, they were immediately deported from Cambodia, as they broke the moral values of this Buddhist state.

Chapter 5 – Jayavarman VII

Bust of King Jayavarman VII as Buddha

https://en.wikipedia.org/wiki/Jayavarman_ VII#/media/File:JayavarmanVII.jpg

The evidence suggests that Suryavarman II led a campaign in Vietnam as late as 1150, but it is unknown when he exactly died. There are no inscriptions preserved from the period between 1145 and 1182, so the history of this period must be reconstructed from what the later kings left behind. It is believed that one of Suryavarman's cousins staged a coup d'état and took the throne. His name was Dharanindravarman II (r. c. 1150–1160), and it appears he was a Buddhist. But it is unclear if he ever ruled from Yasodharapura. According to one inscription dated to Jayavarman VII, Dharanindravarman was succeeded by Yasovarman II. This inscription tells how Yasovarman II put an end to the rebellion somewhere in the north, but it remains a mystery who the people who rebelled were. In the bas-relief of Banteay Chhmar, they were depicted as people with animal heads. This led scholars to believe that the revolt was directed by those who belonged to the bottom of society. This was probably why they were depicted in such a way, as they were the lowest of the low. To the elites, these people would have been on the same level as animals.

Instability in the Khmer Empire continued throughout the 1160s, for it seems Yasovarman II was assassinated by one of his subordinates, Tribhuvanadityavarman, who proceeded to declare himself a king. There is also the absence of inscriptions from this period, which can only be explained by rapid changes and the questionable legitimacy of the rulers. This instability may be a result of the faltering of the hydraulic organization of the kingdom. The system of reservoirs and canals, which were the basis of Angkor's rice economy, started diminishing during the reign of Suryavarman II. Even Angkor Wat was built with much smaller hydraulic components than those of earlier temples. Hydraulic-based cities were still built in the mid-12th century but at a considerable distance from Angkor, at Beng Mealea and Kompong Svay. It is believed that the water sources of the Angkor region were exhausted due to population growth. Even the network of streams and canals that brought water from Phnom Kulen was diverted to supply the ever-growing population. This means that by the time water reached the fields, it was deprived of all the nutrients needed to grow rice. During the dry periods, these canals were probably dried out or became bodies of stagnant water. This stagnation might have even brought malaria upon the citizens of the Angkor region, further destabilizing the kingdom. However, since there is no written evidence, these theories are just speculations.

Jayavarman VII (r. 1811-1218)

Jayavarman VII was the son of Dharanindravarman II and Queen Sri Jayarajacudamani. However, it seems that Jayavarman wasn't a completely legitimate successor to the throne, as he felt compelled to make inscriptions explaining his early life or at least what he wanted the people to believe of his life. Nevertheless, some scholars believed that he was the pinnacle of Khmer kingship despite his less legitimate claim to the throne. The inscriptions Jayavarman VII left behind tell us about his radical changes and his departure from tradition. It is because of this radicalism that Jayavarman VII dominates the historiography of Cambodia.

Like his father, Jayavarman was a Buddhist. He may have been a cousin of Suryavarman II, as he also belonged to the so-called Mahidharapura dynasty. However, some scholars doubt Jayavarman was the son of Dharanindravarman because this fact is very poorly documented. Nevertheless, Jayavarman did serve a role in the court of Yasovarman, but between 1166 and 1177, he lived away from the Angkor region. A statue of him in the Preah Kham temple in Kompong Svay, where the city of Jayadityapura is located, was found, and it is dated to the period before his reign. Maybe that is where he spent those years away from Angkor. But there is also evidence that he spent some time in Champa. This makes some scholars think that Jayadityapura was a rival city of Angkor or maybe its vassal. The questions of how Jayavarman was related to the usurper king Tribhuvanadityavarman, who came after Yasovarman, and what he was doing in Champa remain unanswered.

Jayavarman was a Buddhist king, and he followed the teachings of Mahayana Buddhism. He did his best to integrate Buddhist beliefs with the Cambodian kingship doctrines. Therefore, he practiced Buddhist kingship, which was different in several ways from the Hindu kingship Khmer was used to. In Hinduism, it is believed that a king, dead or alive, enjoyed a particular relationship with one of the Hindu deities, whether that was Shiva, Vishnu, or the composite of the two known as Harihara. The king would always dedicate his temple mountain to the deity he revered, and the kings used this special relationship with the gods to explain their power and grandeur. But the people believed that their power was what secured their relationship with the divine and thus secured regular rainfall. This was why Cambodians believed a king was necessary. Due to his ability to talk to the gods, the king had to be isolated. He distanced himself from the people and locked himself in his grand palace. He was both the master and victim of this kingship system. He enjoyed the power and wealth, and he was the central figure to whom the people pled for favors, titles, and rights. But he was alone, and he rarely had the welfare of his people in mind when making decisions, as he had to work for the benefit of the kingdom as a whole, which most of the time meant exploiting his subjects.

The Buddhist kingdom grew out of the Hindu model (after all, Buddha was an Indian prince), but some of the elements of the rule were modified under Jayavarman VII. The king was no longer seen as having a special relationship with one of the gods, and he would not join the divines after his death. Instead, Jayavarman believed that he needed to redeem himself through devotion to Buddhist teachings and through the performance of good deeds. Still, Jayavarman never sought to deconstruct the Cambodian belief system or get rid of the existing social structures. He didn't ban

Hindu institutions, such as Brahmanism, slavery, or even kingship. He was extremely tolerant of Hinduism, and he used it to build his vision of kingship. After all, he was a 12th-century king, and slavery and social discord were a norm at that time.

The main difference between the Hindu and Buddhist kingships was how the ruler viewed his subjects. In Hindu tradition, the king performed various rituals, built temples, arranged marriages, and produced inscriptions and poems that celebrated his grandeur and godliness. But he did all of this without an audience. People were devoid of the knowledge of what lay behind the rituals and what was in the poems and inscriptions. To the king, the number of his subjects was what mattered most. The more people he ruled, the greater a king he was. Buddhist kings, on the other hand, used their subjects as an audience, objects of their compassion, and as the element of their redemption. It was through his subjects and by performing good deeds that a Buddhist king could redeem his soul from the misdeeds of his past lives.

Jayavarman was married to Princess Jayarajadevi, and after her death, he married her sister, Indradevi. It is believed that these two women were the main influences on not only his devotion to Buddhism but also his reign. However, some scholars believe that an event that preceded Jayavarman's coronation determined the course of his reign. This was the invasion of Champa in 1177, and Jayavarman's whole reign was a response to this attack. It was mentioned earlier that Jayavarman spent some time during the 1160s in Champa. This fact has led historians to believe that the young Jayavarman was out of favor with the Cambodian court, where he had previously served. Maybe he was even exiled. This suggestion is backed by the fact that he dared to come back to Angkor only after the death of Yasovarman II. Even in later inscriptions, Jayavarman rarely speaks of the events of his formative years, which might mean that he had nothing to boast about.

The reasons why Champa attacked Cambodia are elusive because the inscriptions tend to make the connection between any aggressiveness with neighbors to royal ambitions, treachery, and revenge. In 1177, King Jaya Indravarman IV of Champa attacked Cambodia by land, and a year later, he invaded by water, sailing his fleet up the Mekong River. They crossed the Tonle Sap Lake and used the tributary Siem Reap River to approach Yasodharapura. King Tribhuvanadityavarman was killed, and the city was pillaged. One of the inscriptions mentions that King Jaya Indravarman didn't want to listen to any peace proposals. Jayavarman VII took the opportunity to lead the Khmer defensive army, and they managed to expel the invaders from the kingdom. The bas-relief of the Bayon and Banteay Chhmar depict the naval battle between Jayavarman and the Champa army. Although Jayavarman claimed he killed Jaya Indravarman, some of the inscriptions suggest it was another Khmer prince.

Finally, when Jayavarman arrived in Angkor after the invasion, he found the region in disorder. The factions were fighting between themselves and supporting different candidates for the throne. The people also took the opportunity of anarchy to steal and plunder. One of Jayavarman's wives left an inscription in which she claims how before her husband's rule, the land was divided between many rulers and suffered greatly from this fracture. She further describes how Jayavarman united the people under his own rule and brought security and stability to the kingdom. Jayavarman was crowned king between 1181 and 1183 (the exact date is unknown). The kingdom he inherited was ruined thanks to his immediate predecessors, but through his faith, victories in battles, and his ability to judge justly, Jayavarman liberated Angkor from its past. However, the period between the victory over Champa and his coronation is empty, devoid of any inscriptions. It must have been a period of political negotiations and maybe even further conflicts with local chieftains. Once Jayavarman was on the throne, he wanted to reform the kingdom, and he saw himself as the main instrument of this transformation.

The building program of Jayavarman VII was a hasty one. He built a lot and fast. He built everything, from roads to temples to reservoirs. Many of the projects he started had to be finished after his death, but because he built so much and so fast, most of the buildings were done sloppily. He also used up the local supplies of limestone and sandstone, which had been used in building Angkor Wat. His inscriptions say that thousands of people worked on his building projects. Furthermore, it concludes that Jayavarman thought that labor would remove his people from the suffering in which they were entrenched. Although he didn't specify what exactly that suffering was, he did mention that he could feel the physical pain of his subjects. He felt this as spiritual pain; therefore, it was on a higher level, meaning he felt more than his own subjects did. This is in accordance with the Buddhist teachings, which places suffering as related to a purpose in life. Physical suffering is less important because it's just that—physical.

Jayavarman appears to be a compassionate king due to this belief, but did Jayavarman have only the best interests of his people in mind at all times? There is a certain duality in his persona and in the depictions of him as a king. All the bas-relief scenes that depict his battle against the Chams show him as a ruthless, bloodthirsty, and almost tyrannical leader. But his statues and the inscriptions that mention him depict him as a calm, serene, and wise man who lived an ascetic life. The extensive roadbuilding that he performed may have been connected with the military expeditions he engaged, but it also may have been that the roads were needed for easier transport of goods to port towns and China. However, Jayavarman was also in his late fifties when he took the throne, and it might be that he built extensively and with haste because he was racing against time. He wanted to leave behind at least as much as his predecessors, if not even more, but he had considerably less time to do so.

Not much is known about the early years of Jayavarman's reign, except that he considerably expanded the kingdom. It is believed that this expansion helped him gain the support of elite classes, as the Brahmins were aware of the benefits the expansion brought to the kingdom. By the beginning of the 13th century, Laos, Thailand, and Champa were paying tribute to Angkor, which was an enormous accomplishment for a new king, especially one who had started from the low position of a simple court official and one who had probably been disfavored too. However, his accomplishments brought him the support of at least part of the people. There was an uprising in the north that had to be dealt with, but other than that, Jayavarman ruled his kingdom without much internal trouble. However, he was a Buddhist king, and his Hindu elite class must have felt some kind of resentment toward him. This is especially seen in the anti-Buddhist iconoclasm that occurred in Cambodia after Jayavarman's death.

Jayavarman was also an innovative king. He was the first one to build hospitals, constructing around 102 of them. According to the stele of Ta Prohm, the first four were built at the gates of Angkor Thom, as well as to the west of Angkor in the area of modern-day northeastern Thailand. Some were even built as far as today's Laos. The hospitals served 838 villages, and steles were carved upon the foundation of the hospitals, which give details about their administration. Unlike his predecessors, Jayavarman gave special notice to public works. While earlier kings mentioned only the building of reservoirs as public works, Jayavarman thought that the construction of roads, hospitals, and bridges was equally important. Another important public construction work of Jayavarman's reign was the "houses of fire." The exact purpose of these buildings is unknown, but it may be that they served as rest houses for travelers. They were built in ten-mile intervals along the roads. There were fifty-seven "houses of fire" on the road that connected the capitals of the Khmer Empire and Champa.

The Temples of Jayavarman VII

Just like his Hindu predecessors, Jayavarman dedicated the second half of his reign to building temples in honor of his parents. The first one was built in 1186 and is called Ta Phom ("ancestor Brahma"). It was erected to honor the king's mother, who was depicted as Prajnaparamita, the goddess of wisdom, a central concept of Mahayana Buddhism. The temple also had a statue of Jayavarman's guru, a Buddhist teacher. This statue was surrounded by more than six hundred statues of Buddhist gods and bodhisattvas (enlightened creatures). The Buddhist temples of Jayavarman also include cells for Shaivite and Vaishnavite ascetics, right along with the dwelling cells of Buddhist monks. Ta Prohm was never restored, and it mostly lays in ruins today. It is hard to imagine what it must have looked like and what it symbolized during its glory days. Today, this temple is overgrown, with tree roots entwined around its columns, walls, and gates. It is one of the most mysterious places on Earth, and it awakens the imagination of the people.

Preah Khan ("sacred sword") was the next temple built by Jayavarman VII. The inscription of the temple mentions it was built on the site of an important battle against the Chams. Its name during the reign of Jayavarman was Jayasri ("victory and throne"), probably to symbolize the event. However, no other inscriptions mention this battle, although it is possible it was a later Cham invasion, one in which they came close to Yasodharapura but didn't manage to take it. Preah Khan was built in 1191, and it is a temple that honors Jayavarman's father, Dharanindravarman, who is depicted as Lokesvara, the deity expressing the compassion of the Buddha. The symbolism is extremely important here. In Mahayana Buddhism, wisdom and compassion united to give birth to enlightenment. Since Jayavarman's mother was depicted as wisdom and his father as the embodiment of compassion, the king was born enlightened. This trinity of wisdom, compassion, and enlightenment was central to Jayavarman's religious thinking, and these figures started popping up all around the kingdom during his reign. Even the location of the temples is symbolic. They were placed northeast and southeast of Yasodharapura's new center, Angkor Thom, which suggests that compassion and wisdom united in Yasodharapura, giving enlightenment to the land. There, in the new capital of Angkor Thom, was the Bayon Temple, which housed this enlightenment in the form of a Buddha statue.

The inscriptions on these two temples prove the magnitude of Jayavarman's kingdom, but they also show us how Cambodian bureaucracy developed, especially in terms of states' control over the duties of the population. Ta Prohm housed several thousand people, as the inscription there describes the existence of 18 high priests, 2,740 other priests, 2,232 assistants, and 12,640 people. Additionally, there were 66,625 men and women who performed services. Among them were also Burmese, Chams, and other ethnic groups who came to Cambodia. In total, there were 79,265 people around this temple. Preah Khan had a similar inscription, stating that over 100,000 people were drawn to the area from 5,300 neighboring villages. The outsiders, such as the Burmese and Chams, were accounted for differently than the Khmer population. Maybe they were prisoners or slaves gained in wars, but it is clear they had no ties to noblemen or religious institutions.

Although the temples were Buddhist, they also housed learned Hindu men and the statues of Hindu gods. Jayavarman approved of this arrangement, as he was aware that the majority of his subjects were Hindu. The temple inscriptions also mention that 13,500 villages were previously dependent on the temple sites back when they were Hindu sacred places. This means that, in total, the temple served around 300,000 people, both Buddhists and Hindu.

At the center of the new capital was the Bayon Temple. Its original name was Jayagiri ("victory mountain"), but it was renamed in the 19th century because of its obvious Buddhist imagery. The temple itself is rich with gigantic portrait imagery and bas-reliefs depicting the wars with Champa, the Indian gods, and scenes from everyday life. However, many of these were added later when the Khmer Empire reverted back to Hinduism. Primarily, the Bayon was built as a Buddhist temple. Its central statue was of Buddha shielded by a giant snake or naga. But this statue, found in the 1930s, was no longer in its original place. It was removed during the iconoclastic period after Jayavarman's death and thrown into an air shaft. Interestingly, the bas-relief scenes of the Bayon Temple depict historical scenes rather than the mythological ones taken from the *Ramayana* and *Mahabharata*. The battles that were depicted show the standard weaponry of 12th-century Cambodia. Other segments of the reliefs show the common people buying and selling items, eating, picking fruit, taking care of children, healing the sick, traveling, and gambling, among other activities. Interestingly, these scenes, including the costumes, artifacts, and customs depicted, could be encountered in the Cambodian countryside at the end of the colonial period (Cambodia gained self-rule in 1946).

After Jayavarman's rule, Cambodian history started its period of silence. Not many inscriptions were produced, and those that were rarely even mentioned Jayavarman VII. This historical silence began during the last years of Jayavarman's reign, which might mean that he is to be blamed for it somehow. He did, after all, break the patterns of continuity evident in the rulers before him. This silence is also reflected in the sudden stop of building projects. However, maybe the inscriptions still need to be found. Only time will tell if there is more to be learned about the reign of Jayavarman VII. After him, wide-ranging social and ideological changes occurred, and they continued throughout the rest of the 13th century and through the 14th century. These changes might have been set in motion by Jayavarman himself, but it is most likely that it was his descendants' doing.

Chapter 6 – The Crisis of the 13th Century

Angkor Wat

https://en.wikipedia.org/wiki/Angkor_Wat#/media/File:Ankor_Wat_temple.jpg

After the death of Jayavarman VII, Cambodia went through radical ideological changes. The throne was succeeded by Jayavarman's son, Indravarman II, but little is known about him, for his successor, Jayavarman VIII, destroyed all his inscriptions. It is believed that Indravarman ruled in relative peace, finished the temples his father started building, and died in 1243.

The biggest change that was brought about wasn't of a royal nature but of a religious one. Jayavarman was a Mahayana Buddhist, but during his reign, Theravada Buddhism truly entered the kingdom. The presence of this sect had been in existence in Cambodia for centuries, but it was always neglected and pushed aside as a non-dominant religion. But something changed during the 13th century, as the majority of people openly converted to it. Jayavarman VIII sent one of his sons, Tamalinda, to Sri Lanka to study Theravada Buddhism and to be ordained as a monk. Tamalinda returned to Angkor and started spreading the Theravada branch of Buddhism, but it isn't likely that this mass conversion was the deed of just one man. Other wandering missionaries from Siam, Burma, and Sri Lanka also visited Angkor.

But what compelled people to suddenly change their religion? Some historians believe Theravada Buddhism was oriented toward the benefits of the common people, and because of it, the majority of the population found it easy to identify with the new religion. Others claim it was the pressure of the Mongol invasion of China that pushed the Southeast Asian nations to convert to Theravada Buddhism as it was a more militant sect. However, the most probable explanation for the sudden and fast conversion of the Khmer population could be very simple. During the expansion years of Jayavarman VII, the Khmer increased their interaction with the Mon-speaking population of northern Thailand, who were already devotees of Theravada Buddhism. Theravada Buddhism became the dominant religion, and even though it was replaced by Hinduism later, it reestablished itself. To this day, it is the official religion of Cambodia, with more than 98 percent of the citizens identifying as Theravada Buddhists.

The conversion of people in the 13th century was not total. It was fast-paced and took place on a massive scale, but it took at least half a century to establish itself as a dominant religion. When the Chinese ambassador Zhou Daguan visited Angkor in 1296, he noticed that Brahmanism and Shamanism were still very much alive, and they were also the officially approved religions next to Theravada Buddhism. But there is a huge lack of evidence regarding the 13th century in Cambodia. Possibly it was marked by a series of religious upheavals that left a certain effect on the political life of the Empire of Angkor.

The spread of Theravada Buddhism wasn't the only change that occurred in Cambodia during the 13th century. The Mongolian invasion of China shook the whole region, and a rapid and significant movement of people occurred. Foreign innovations entered the kingdom, and trade changed its well-established patterns. It is unknown if these changes were just a consequence of the general adoption of the new faith, but it is known that Brahmins, although they retained their court positions, lost their significance. With the decline of Hinduism, the bas-reliefs on the temples changed to suit Theravada Buddhism narratives. The scenes of local versions of the *Ramayana* and *Mahabharata* were replaced with images that depicted Buddhist values. Literature and iconography also changed, as well as sculptures, architecture, and the various inscriptions the kings left behind.

During the 13th century, Cambodia developed its foreign relations in two very different ways. Its grasp over the population of northern Thailand weakened, and it accepted Chinese commercial activities in Cambodian territory. Because of the Mongol expansion, China, under the early Ming dynasty, sought to expand its trade on Southeast Asian soil. However, the Chinese failed to assert their cultural influence, and the Cambodian culture remained dominant. However, Cambodian political influence over the region diminished. Some of the principalities that sent tribute to Angkor declared their independence, and to symbolize this transition, they sent tributes to the Chinese throne instead. The first to do so were Sukhothai and Louvo. In time, Laos and other principalities in the south followed their example. Angkor became vulnerable to foreign attacks from all sides, except the east, where the weakened Champa was no longer in power. A Thai invasion occurred sometime at the end of the 13th century. The Chinese ambassador Zhou Daguan recorded it.

Zhou Daguan in Angkor (1296-1297)

The most detailed account of life in 13th-century Cambodia was left behind by the Chinese ambassador named Zhou Daguan. He stayed in Angkor from August 1296 to sometime in 1297, during which time he wrote down his thoughts and described the appearance of Angkor. As he was not constrained by the Indian traditional belief system, he was free to describe the life of the Khmer in detail, such as bathing, trading, and marching in procession. Hindu tradition was always more concerned with the royal and divine, leaving out everyday life events. For Zhou, the Khmer were barbaric as well as exotic, and he was fascinated by their way of life. This was why he devoted his manuscript to them instead of the historical facts that we today miss. Zhou's memoirs don't reveal what happened during the years of rapid change in Cambodian society, but they do give us an insight into how the common people lived, what they did, and how they saw the world around them. Zhou's account of Cambodia is very short. Translated in English, it numbers only forty pages. It is divided into various topics, such as religion, kingship, justice, customs, slaves, vegetables, and birds, just to name a few. Incredibly, certain facets described by the Chinese envoy were still around in 20th-century Cambodia, including slavery, trial by ordeal, and sumptuary laws, though in modified form.

Five of the sections in Zhou's text deal with religion, kingship, slavery, festivals, and the king's excursions. From them, we can see that in the 13th century, Cambodia had three official religions: Brahmanism, Theravada Buddhism, and Shaivism. Zhou describes the Brahmins, saying they often occupied high offices of the court, but he couldn't say much about their religion. Zhou noticed the lack of Brahmanism schools and books from which they learned, and he never found out what was the source of their doctrine. Theravada Buddhists were more or less the same as they are today. According to Zhou, they shaved their heads, dressed in yellow robes, leaving their right shoulder exposed, and walked barefooted. He also describes Buddhist monasteries, saying that they had tile roofs, just like the houses of the high officials and the royal palace. The ordinary people had their roofs made out of thatch.

Zhou was surprised to discover that the Theravada Buddhist wats (complex of warships that included housing, temples, and schools) lacked bells, flags, cymbals, and platforms. They were much simpler than the Mahayana Buddhist temples of China. But these temples did contain a figure of Buddha, which was made out of gilded plaster. Zhou then describes the process of inscribing the sacred and historical texts on the palm leaf, a practice that survived well into the 20th century.

Zhou then describes the Shaivites. He called them "followers of the Dao" because he thought their doctrine was similar to Daoism (or Taoism). According to the Chinese ambassador, the Shaivites occupied monasteries much less prosperous than the Buddhist ones. They prayed and left offerings to no icon, and they only used a block of stone to serve as their altar. Shaivism declined after the abandonment of Angkor, and it soon disappeared, but Hindu practices and cults, including the use of lingams, continued to exist, even in modern times.

When describing the people of Angkor, Zhou noticed that many of them served in some form of slavery. People who had many slaves had more than a hundred. Those who had few slaves had anywhere between ten and twenty. The poor people, as one might expect, had no slaves. He mentioned that the slaves were usually taken from the mountain tribes. This was common in Cambodia even during the 19th century. Slaves were set apart from the rest of the people by prohibitions. They could sit and sleep only under the house, never inside. The only time a slave was allowed to enter the house was when they were performing a task. Even then, they had to kneel and bow to the floor, greeting the house and its owner before they could continue forward. The slaves had no civil privileges, and the kingdom didn't even recognize their marriages. They were forced to refer to their owners as fathers and mothers, but they were not welcomed as part of the family. The slaves constantly tried to escape, but if they were caught, they were marked by tattoos or mutilation.

Unfortunately, Zhou failed to describe the proportions of the Khmer society. We don't know if slaves or free but poor people were the majority. He rarely referred to the middle class, which existed (they owned a few slaves), or the private landowners. There were also Sino-Cambodians who were active in domestic and foreign trade. The religious figures were given special privileges, and the slaves had special prohibitions, but it remains a mystery who were the common people of the Khmer Empire. Who were the people in between, the ones without privileges or restrictions? Who were the people who made the kingdom prosper?

Next, Zhou described the celebration of New Year, which took place in November. This marked the end of the rainy season when the agricultural year started. This ceremony became known as the "Water Festival" after the 15th century when the kingdom moved the capital to Phnom Penh. Even then, it was celebrated in a similar way as described by Zhou. Big plateaus were erected from which fireworks were launched. The king and the elite families were the patrons of the celebration, and the king himself would come out to watch the fireworks. The ceremony was celebrated in Cambodia until 1970, when the monarchy was overthrown. Both the ceremony and the monarchy were reinstated in 1993.

Zhou also noticed that the Khmer had three to four rice harvests per year. However, this is very unlikely for the whole country. It was probably like that in the developed region of Angkor, where all the manpower was concentrated. The Angkor region is also known for fertile alluvial soil and for an advanced watering system, which had been perfected over several hundred years. Zhou continues to describe how Cambodia had rain for six months and then no rain for another six months. It rained every day from April until September, and during these months, the nearby Tonle Sap Lake would swell up with accumulated water. Zhou describes how, at its highest, the lake would completely cover the trees, and only their tips could be seen emerging from the water. People who lived on the banks of the lake had to move to the hills during the rainy season. The lake would dry during the months between October and March, during which time there was not a drop of rain. The boats had trouble navigating the low waters of Tonle Sap, and only the smallest and the lightest were able to cross it.

The "miracle" of Tonle Sap amazed many 19th-century travelers to Cambodia. During the dry season, the waters retreated and left behind very rich nutrients for the soil. Even after the abandonment of Angkor, the lake remained one of the most densely inhabited water surfaces in the world. Zhou was amazed by the waterworks of the Khmer Empire, but he never bothered to explain the agriculture of the land in detail. We still have many questions. How was the rice surplus handled? How much land was owned by the royal family? How much was owned by the Brahmins or Buddhist monasteries? Who were the people who cultivated the land? Were they free or slaves? But there are no answers to these questions. However, Zhou did write about Angkor markets, and astonishingly, they resemble the Cambodian markets we know today. Zhou explains that of the locals who traded, all were women. Market day was every day, and the market was open from six in the morning until noon. The products that were for sale were displayed on tumbleweed mats laid on the ground. The traders had to pay rental fees to the royal officials to use the designated mats as their selling points.

By the 13th century, many Chinese came to Cambodia to trade, and many of them even settled in Cambodia. Zhou describes that the products exported by Khmer were more or less the same as the ones during the Funan era. Beeswax, ivory, pepper, feathers, cardamom, and lacquer were the main items Cambodians exported until the 20th century. They imported ceramics, paper, metal goods, wicker, silk, and porcelain. It is unclear how the government paid for these products, but there is no evidence of Cambodians using any currency. Zhou never mentioned if Cambodians paid in kind or if they used any money.

Zhou was fascinated with the king of Angkor, Indravarman III (r. 1295-1308), and how he succeeded the throne. He said that the new king was the son-in-law of the old king, Jayavarman VIII. Upon the abdication of the old king, his daughter, Srindrabhupesvarachuda, stole her father's golden sword and presented it to her husband, thus making him a king and denying the title from Jayavarman VIII's son, her brother. The new king, according to Zhou, had a secret piece of metal sewn under his skin so that no arrow or knife could hurt him. Protected like this, he was able to leave his palace any time he wanted. Zhou wasn't in Angkor when the new king came to power, but these events were the stories he heard. Some of these events are discreetly described in inscriptions dated to the reign of Indravarman III. The Chinese ambassador also describes how the king would leave his palace. All of his soldiers would gather in front of the king, and the procession was followed by the people, who waved banners, as well as by musicians and drummers. The women of the palace would also come out, anywhere between three hundred and five hundred of them. They wore coiled-up hair-dos and were dressed in floral designs. They carried huge candles that were lit even during the day.

Some women carried exotic instruments and gold and silver utensils from the palace, but their purpose is unknown, as it seems they didn't play on those instruments or eat and drink during the procession. Another contingent was made out of women who wore lances and shields. The relatives of the king, ministers, and high officials were at the front of the procession, and they rode elephants. They also carried red parasols. The king was behind them, and he would stand on his elephant. He carried a sword made out of gold in his hand, and he was shielded by twenty white parasols laced with gold.

Zhou concluded that even though Cambodia was the land of barbarians, the people knew that their ruler was supreme.

Chapter 7 – The Abandonment of Angkor and Cambodia after the Angkorian Period

Henri Mouhot's drawing entitled Facade of Angkor Wat *(1860)*

https://en.wikipedia.org/wiki/Angkor_Wat#/media/File:Facade_of_Angkor_Wat.jpg

Jayavarman VII was the last good king of the Khmer Empire. After his reign, the whole empire hurled into decline, eventually ending by the 15th century. Jayavarman was succeeded by Indravarman II, who, in turn, was succeeded by Jayavarman VIII. Nothing is known about Indravarman II, probably because his successor destroyed his inscriptions and statues. Jayavarman VIII (r. 1243-1295) was a Hindu king, and he was merciless toward the rising Theravada Buddhism. The Empire of Angkor was attacked by the Mongol forces, which were led by the famous Kublai Khan, during this period. It is believed that Jayavarman survived this attack because he paid the Mongols and bought peace in 1283. When Indravarman III succeeded the throne, he restored Theravada Buddhism as the state religion. A series of unremarkable kings followed, as well as more religious changes. The empire would shift from Buddhism to Hinduism, depending on the religious views of the kings who succeeded the Angkor throne. This is also the last recorded period of the Khmer Empire. It falls between Zhou's visit to Angkor and a king named Chan, who is remembered for restoring some of the old temples during the 1550s and 1560s. The centuries in between witnessed major shifts in the Angkor economy, language, foreign relations, and the structure of Cambodian society.

Inscriptions from this period are very rare. There is some evidence that comes from within the kingdom from the mid-14th century. The rest is taken from Chinese records, Cham sources, and some inscriptions from Thailand. The Thai records of the 17th century do contain some information on the political and economic conditions of the last years of the Empire of Angkor. The Cambodian chronicles, which were written much later, refer to the period but draw from folklore and the Thai chronicles. Nothing new can be learned from them. It seems that the Chinese records are the most reliable when it comes to the end of the Angkorian era. This is probably because the changes in the Cambodian political, economic, and social systems were made because of

Chinese influence and their extensive trade with Southeast Asia under the Mongols and the Ming dynasty. Between 1371 and 1432, more than twenty-one embassies were sent to the Ming court, which was more than during the whole Angkorian period, probably because of the fast-developing trade between the two countries. Some of these missions were ceremonial or maybe were sent to ask China for support against common enemies. But the majority of these missions were due to trade, and the respect Cambodians received from the Chinese only testifies that Angkor was still a very influential kingdom in the region.

The Cambodian elite was now more relaxed since the old ceremonial duties of Brahmanical bureaucracy were dying out. The whole society was less rigid and probably more open to the idea of trade with neighboring kingdoms. There is no way of telling how and why this shift in Cambodian thinking and behavior occurred, but scholars believe that it wasn't the decline of the kingdom that brought about this change. Just the fact that the Cambodians were able to convince the Chinese that they were still relevant in the region speaks about the low possibilities of a sudden and catastrophic decline of Angkor. Recent studies have shown that the Angkor region was still heavily populated during the 14th and 15th centuries, and the local kings were able to compete for resources. Some older buildings in Angkor were even restored during the 15th and 16th centuries, further testifying that the region was important. There is even evidence that the occupants of the Angkor region warred with Thai peoples and with the Ayutthaya Kingdom to the west during the 17th century. Although this was no longer the Khmer Empire, the fact that the region was inhabited at the time is evidence enough for the continuity of the kingdom.

Scholars also believe the Empire of Angkor might have gradually declined, pointing to the lack of evidence as support for their argument. There were only around one hundred inscriptions found belonging to the period between the 13th and 15th centuries, whereas before, there were around one thousand inscriptions made per century. This period also lacked the construction of new temples, water systems, or grandiose reservoirs. But that doesn't necessarily mean the kingdom declined. Maybe *change* and *transformation* are better terms. Cambodia continued to be a strong state, but it wouldn't have been so if the Empire of Angkor declined. But it is understandable why we are inclined to speak of decline. The kings of the period between the 14th and 15th centuries abandoned Angkor and shifted their center toward other cities, closer to the trade routes with China. However, that doesn't mean Angkor itself was completely abandoned. It continued to thrive as a city, just not as the capital city. With the royal abandonment of the city, the majority of the population moved too. Scholars argue that Angkor suddenly found itself without enough people to maintain its complex irrigation network. If they allowed the waters of the Angkor region to become stagnant, malaria-carrying mosquitos would become abundant. The population would be further depleted, which would eventually lead to the complete abandonment of the region.

Some scholars believe that the conversion to Theravada Buddhism brought changes to the nation that led to the decline of the kingdom. They used the very nature of Buddhism to explain how Angkor kings lost some territories. However, some of the neighboring people, such as the Thai and Burmese, also belonged to the Theravada Buddhism branch and were prosperous kingdoms at this time. Scholars have so far failed to connect these military victories with the pacifist nature of Buddhism. Still, many things changed within the Empire of Angkor due to the mass conversion to Theravada Buddhism. Angkorian institutions, such as inscriptions, temples, and the Hindu royal family, came to a stop or were redirected to serve a Buddhist narrative. But these social changes were not the result of religious changes exclusively. The neighboring Theravada kingdom of Ayutthaya was rising in power, so people moved there. They brought with them Angkorian ideas, texts, and traditions, and these were then modified only to be reintroduced to Cambodia in their new version. In 1431, the Thai invasion of Angkor occurred, and more people, who had been taken as war prisoners, were moved to the west. Due to the foreign invasion, the local people and the royal family moved to Phnom Penh, where they reestablished the capital of Cambodia. The capital of Cambodia is still located there today.

Phnom Penh was a suitable location for the new capital because it lies on the confluence of the Mekong and Tonle Sap. The city had existed since the 5th century CE, and it gradually developed to become a fortified city by the late 14th century. Its position was perfect for food trade operations that were flourishing with China. Cambodians would approach the Mekong Delta, which was still under Khmer control, and trade with merchants from China and Laos. Because of this, making Phnom Penh the new capital was an economic move, and as the kingdom developed its trade, it was also a logical move. The move to Phnom Penh might also have been motivated by personal or regional gains of the members of the royal family. Later, this move was legitimized, but the people left behind in Angkor were abandoned to fend for themselves in a declining empire, suffering the attacks of the neighboring kingdoms. To legitimize the move of the capital from Angkor to Phnom Penh, a myth of the city's foundation was developed. A lady named Penh found a floating tree in the waters of Tonle Sap. She pulled it out on the shore and found four figures of Buddha and one of Vishnu inside of the tree. This was a symbol that the area was blessed and that it would prosper under the patronage of both Buddhist and Hindu deities.

The new capital's importance to trade is mirrored in the abundant presence of foreigners. Phnom Penh housed Malay speakers from Champa and the islands of Indonesia. They influenced the Khmer language and left behind words such as *kompong* ("landing place") and *psar* ("market"). The Malay legacy in Cambodia still needs to be researched, for it seems that it runs deeper. The descriptions of 17th-century Cambodian political systems strongly resemble the one that existed in riverine Malaya at the time. Other foreigners who left their mark on the new capital were the Chinese. In the 1540s, there were three thousand Chinese living in Phnom Penh, and they started intermarrying into the Cambodian elite families.

The previous social organization, bureaucracy, and economic priorities of Angkor heavily depended on slavery and forced labor. However, by the end of the 15th century, these were no longer relevant. Nor was the heavy taxation of the people and their divide into the castes. New forms of social organization entered the kingdom, along with new patterns of settlements and new economic priorities. This was all due to the connections Cambodia developed with its neighbors through trade. The change was on a much larger scale than just the Empire of Angkor. It happened in the whole of Southeast Asia, and by the end of the 16th century, the Empire of Angkor and the rising Ayutthaya Kingdom regarded each other not as separate polities but as common participants in one hybrid culture. This hybrid culture was a mixture of Hinduinized kingship and Theravada principles of monarchy. The old Angkorian ideology met the new Theravada to form a unique civilization. But they also included the remnants of paternalistic village-oriented leadership of the Thai people and tribal peoples of the hills of southern China. The Khmer language was an official language in both kingdoms during the 14th century, and they shared a common religion as well, which was also accessible to ordinary people too. These people came in contact with each other through war, trade, immigration, and their shared religion, and together, they developed a separate cultural tradition, abandoning the old, completely Hinduinized way of life.

Cambodia in the 15th and 16th Centuries

Little is known about the events in the Angkor region immediately after the Thai invasion. It seems that the Thai administration was overthrown by the forces of Phnom Penh sometime in the middle of the 15th century. It is believed that the names of the kings who ruled from Phnom Penh during this period are all fictional, even though they are recorded in local chronicles. However, we know that at the end of the 15th century, a new conflict arose between the local rulers. One of these rulers became the dominant one. Some sources claim he was a former slave, while the European writings of the 19th century claim he was a relative of a former monarch. Nevertheless, he exiled the former king, Chan I, who found refuge in Ayutthaya. But Chan returned to power later and brought with him a Thai army that helped him depose the usurper. Chan's restoration to power under Thai patronage was seen as a bad omen, and the eastern provinces, from where the usurper hailed, remained rebellious. From the 1620s onward, they often sought help from their Vietnamese neighbors.

A Cambodian chronicle mentions that a Khmer king married a Vietnamese princess in the 1630s and allowed the Vietnamese people to establish a base in the Mekong Delta. By that time, the Mekong Delta was still predominantly inhabited by the Khmer but was outside of Cambodia's direct control. The next two hundred years saw Vietnamese immigrants pouring into the region and taking full administrative control over it. Even today, Cambodians call this region Lower Cambodia or Kampuchea Krom, and the Khmer people are a significant part of the Vietnamese culture that developed in the region. The Thai presence in the north and the Vietnamese presence to the east created a competitive atmosphere for dominance over the Cambodian court. The people were divided into those who supported the Thai and those who supported the Vietnamese. This factionalism was already very severe in the 1680s, and it stayed like this until the 1860s.

The first European who mentioned Cambodia in his writings was probably Tomé Pires, a Portuguese apothecary. He joined one of the first European expeditions to Southeast Asia, and he wrote *Suma Oriental,* a book on Asian trade. He described the Cambodian kingdom as a warlike one, with a superior ruler who obeyed no one. But Pires was relying on hearsay when he hinted about the riches that could be gained from Cambodia. He never really visited the state but rather collected the stories from merchants and mariners in the ports of India and China. The first European who was an eyewitness to 16th-century Cambodia was a Portuguese missionary named Gaspar da Cruz. He visited Longvek during the reign of King Chan I in 1556. He spent only one year there, as he was unable to convert the Khmer to Christianity. He blamed the strong influence of Buddhism and the superstition of the Khmer people. However, he did describe the loyalty of the Cambodian people to their king. According to Cruz, the people dared do nothing without the king's approval, and they were unable to make complicated decisions without their ruler. Cruz also described how more than a third of able-bodied Cambodians were part of the *sangha,* a Buddhist community of monks and nuns. He also mentioned that the rest of the population was loyal to the Buddhist monks and even regarded them as living gods.

Cruz was also astonished by the organization of Cambodian society and the role of the king. According to him, if a man of the house died, all his possessions were returned to the king, while his wife and children went off to find a better future somewhere else. They did steal what they could, though. This means that people held possessions only at the king's pleasure, and this went for ranks, land, and social positions as well. This demonstrates that the kingship in the 16th century retained the absolutism of the Angkorian model, even after the mass conversion to Buddhism. Due to this absolutism, the elite families could not unite into opposition to the king, as the king would easily dispose of them.

Cruz never mentioned Angkor, and it is possible he never even knew of its existence or importance.

Conclusion

In 1599, Portuguese writer Diego do Couto visited Cambodia, and he wrote down the stories he heard. One of them described an event that happened some forty years before his arrival to Cambodia (around 1550). The king was on the hunt when he stumbled upon some ruins. He was amazed by the height of the walls he saw, and he ordered his people to cut the vines and branches that were obstructing the entrance to the ruins. Thousands of people worked for several days so that the king could go inside and marvel at the construction of his ancestors. Once he got inside, he was awed by the beauty and craftsmanship of the place and decided to move his court to the ruins and rebuild the whole site. These ruins were the remnants of Angkor, left behind and forgotten by its people. There are no other sources that describe this event, but there are several inscriptions in Angkor dated to the 1560s, which would approximately correspond to the date of its rediscovery. But it is more likely that Angkor was rediscovered during a military campaign, as Cambodia was at war with Siam at the time. The Angkor region was a logical place to station the Cambodian army if an invasion of Siam was planned.

But even though Angkor was once again the capital city of the Khmer, it quickly fell out of use, and the people returned to Phnom Penh. The ruins of Angkor Wat were again discovered in 1860 by a French naturalist named Henri Mouhot. His writings were published three years later, posthumously since he died in Cambodia in 1861. In them, Mouhot described his visit to Angkor and the awe he felt when he first saw the ruins of Angkor Wat. He described how he wondered about the greatness of the past Khmer civilization, which was now, according to him, a barbaric nation. In his native France, the publication was received with awe, and Mouhot was credited with the "discovery of the lost city of Angkor." However, the excitement about this discovery is somewhat controversial as the city was never really lost. The locals knew exactly where it was, and they were aware of its past importance. Mouhot was not even the first foreigner to visit the site. Before him, during the 16th and 17th centuries, Portuguese and Spanish explorers described Angkor and their visits. In the 17th century, the site was even inhabited, mostly by Japanese, who left their inscriptions on the pillars of the city. When Mouhot visited Angkor Wat, there was a settlement on its site, and the place was abundant with life. The better phrasing would be that in 1860, the Western world rediscovered Angkor Wat. And ever since then, the Westerners' interests in Angkor have never ceased.

The same year the writings of Henri Mouhot were published, Cambodia became the protectorate of France. Interest in this new and exotic country only grew. In 1898, the French School of the Far East (EFEO) was founded with the task of studying Cambodia's past, archaeology, art, and language. Thanks to this school, many more ruins in Cambodia were discovered, especially once the usage of LiDAR in archaeology started. Angkor, even though it was still inhabited, was overgrown, and it was damaged by wars and earthquakes. In the early 1900s, the French dedicated much of their funds to the restoration of Angkor Wat and its opening to its first visitors. Since those early days, tourists have been coming to see one of the largest ancient temples on Earth. Mesmerized by its decorations, elaborate bas-reliefs, and statues, many compare it to the works of Renaissance artists. The temple became a UNESCO World Heritage Site in 1992, and it is still a very spiritual place for the Buddhist monks and their followers. For the rest of the world, Angkor is a mysterious and magical place, and its popularity only continues to grow.

Here's another book by Captivating History that you might like

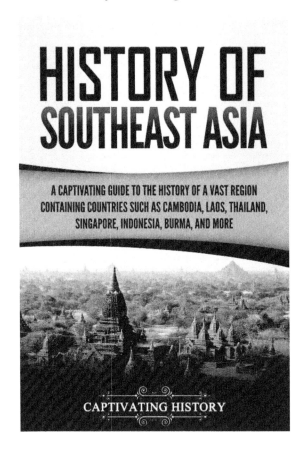

HISTORY OF SOUTHEAST ASIA

A CAPTIVATING GUIDE TO THE HISTORY OF A VAST REGION CONTAINING COUNTRIES SUCH AS CAMBODIA, LAOS, THAILAND, SINGAPORE, INDONESIA, BURMA, AND MORE

CAPTIVATING HISTORY

Free Bonus from Captivating History (Available for a Limited time)

Hi History Lovers!

Now you have a chance to join our exclusive history list so you can get your first history ebook for free as well as discounts and a potential to get more history books for free! Simply visit the link below to join.

Captivatinghistory.com/ebook

Also, make sure to follow us on Facebook, Twitter and Youtube by searching for Captivating History.

Bibliography

"Angkor Dynasty". Retrieved from http://www7.plala.or.jp/seareview/newpage2Chapter4Angkor.html.

"Assassination of Resident General Bardez".

"ASEAN at the Crossroads". Retrieved from https://www.phnompenhpost.com/opinion/asean-crossroads-nam-has-no-alternative.

Cady, J. (1966). *Thailand, Burma, Laos and Cambodia*. New Jersey Press

Cady, J. (1964). *Southeast Asia: Its Historical Development*.

"Cambodia: Achieving the Potential of Urbanization, August 2018". Retrieved from http://documents1.worldbank.org/curated/en/580101540583913800/pdf/127247-REVISED-CambodiaUrbanizationReportEnfinal.pdf.

"Cambodia". Retrieved from http://countrystudies.us/cambodia/6.htm.

"Cambodian Election: Ruling Party Claims Landslide in Vote with No Main Opposition". Retrieved from https://www.bbc.com/news/world-asia-44999358.

Chandler, D. (2009). *A History of Cambodia (4ʰ ed.).* Westview Press.

Coedes, G. (1966). *The Making of Southeast Asia.* New York.

Harrison, B. (1960). *Southeast Asia: A Short History.* London

Karakia, Z. (1973). *Failure through Neglect.*

"Khmer Empire: The Ancient History Encyclopedia". Retrieved from

https://www.ancient.eu/Khmer_Empire/.

Kiernan, B. (2008). *Blood and Soil: Modern-Day Genocide 1500-2000.*

"The Legend of Preah Ko and Preah Keo". Retrieved from

http://arcmthailand.com/documents/documentcenter/THE%20LE
GEND%20OF%20PREAH%20KO%20PREAH%20KEO%20AN
D%20ITS%20INFLUENCE%20ON.pdf.

"Ministry Revises Safe Village Policy". Retrieved from

https://opendevelopmentcambodia.net/news/ministry-revises-safe-
village-commune-policy/#!/story=post-146295.

Stark, M.; Griffin, P.; Phourn, C; Ledgewood, J, et. al. (1999) "Results of the 1995-1996

Archeological Field Investigations at Angkor Borei Asian Perspectives. #38".

"The World Bank Empowering Cambodian Communes". Retrieved from

https://www.worldbank.org/en/news/feature/2011/04/12/empowerin
g-cambodian-communes.

Tarling, N. (1999). *The Cambridge History of Southeast Asia.*

Vickery, M. (2000). *Cambodia 1975-1982.* Silkworm Books.

References

Cambodia - The Khmer state (Angkor). (n.d.). Encyclopedia
Britannica.

https://www.britannica.com/place/Cambodia/The-Khmer-state-
Angkor

Chandler, D. (2007). *A History of Cambodia, 4th Edition (4th ed.)*.
Routledge.

Khmer Empire | Encyclopedia.com. (n.d.). Encyclopedia.

https://www.encyclopedia.com/history/encyclopedias-almanacs-
transcripts-and-maps/khmer-empire

Ortner, J., Mabbett, I. W., Goodman, J., Mabbett, I., Mannikka, E.,
& Sanday, J. (2002).

Angkor: Celestial Temples of the Khmer (1st ed.). Abbeville Press.

Plubins, R. Q. (2021, March 17). Khmer Empire. World History
Encyclopedia.

https://www.ancient.eu/Khmer_Empire/

So, K. T., & So, J. (2017a). *The Khmer Kings and the History of
Cambodia: BOOK I –*

1st Century to 1595: Funan, Chenla, Angkor and Longvek Periods. DatASIA, Inc.

So, K. T., & So, J. (2017b). *The Khmer Kings and the History of Cambodia: BOOK I - 1st Century to 1595: Funan, Chenla, Angkor and Longvek Periods.* DatASIA, Inc.

Printed in Great Britain
by Amazon